COMPREHENSION QUARTERLY 5

CQ

ISSUE A: Asking Questions

GOBS OF GOO

Gobs of Goo

THINK ABOUT: Asking Questions

A4

NONFICTION
After the Spill

Wally, an Oregon beaver, is one of the thousands of creatures that become victims of oil spills.

A10

FICTION
Looking for the Monster

Jamie learns that pranks sometimes backfire. Now he's wondering if he and his friends had a muddy tug-of-war with a *real* monster!

A18

FICTION
Surprise Sunday

A family's Sunday lunch is interrupted in a really **BIG** way—by an erupting volcano!

A24

NONFICTION
Goo Is a Sticky Subject

From maple syrup to snail slime—nature is full of goo!

ASKING QUESTIONS

Getting Involved

Whenever you read something, you become an important part of an author's plan. Careful readers try to figure out what the author intended so they can get the most out of what they read. Often this means **asking questions** about what the author is saying and how he or she says it. Readers ask questions before, during, and after reading to help them better understand what they read.

Jose and Sally are science partners. They have just finished reading a nonfiction article about a local endangered animal, and the article has inspired them to help save the animal. They are discussing how stories like this one might inspire other people to help the environment.

"You know," said Jose, "before I read this article, I thought, not *another* article about some endangered animal. I figured it would be filled with all kinds of depressing facts. But the author started with a cute story about a baby seal. That got me interested. Why do you think she did that?"

Sally replied, "Maybe she did that to get our attention. I knew the author was going to tell us about a serious situation, and I was ready for a lot of information about what we have to do to save seals. But when she described the mother seal trying to take care of her babies in the middle of all that disgusting trash, I really felt sorry for her. I just had to keep reading."

"Yeah!" said Jose. "I noticed she waited until the middle of the article to hit us with the facts. I thought you were supposed to start a news story with the most important information."

Sally said, "Well, I think she started her article with a story that got us involved—you know, that got us to take the subject personally. I think that by the time we were hooked, we were ready to hear the facts and do something about it."

As you read "After the Spill," pay close attention to your mind at work and the questions you have. But most importantly, notice how asking questions about the author's purpose, style, or perspective—and answering those questions—helps you to better understand this article and every story you read!

After the Spill

by Ellen Javernick

Frightened and shivering, the beaver looked around from beneath the dock. The section of the Willamette River the beaver knew as home was bustling with people. He wanted to swim away from the confusion around him, but he was covered in gooey, tar-like gunk. His fur was matted, and his nose and throat were clogged. His body, no longer insulated, was wet and cold.

"Look!" someone shouted. "There's a beaver!" Oil-spill workers rushed to the area. The frightened beaver tried to beat a warning with his tail, but his tail was so heavy with oil that he couldn't lift it.

"We've got to get him help ASAP or he'll die," warned one of the workers. "We may be too late already."

Using a large net, the workers slowly pulled the drenched beaver from beneath the pier. Very weak now, the beaver did not struggle as they wrapped him in blankets and loaded him into the back of a pick-up. The truck raced to a nearby veterinary hospital. Notified in advance that they'd be coming, the veterinarian had contacted the Oregon Fish and Game Department. Preparations for the beaver's arrival were already underway.

Although rescued animals are usually allowed some time to recover before the washing process begins, they could see that this animal needed help fast. The beaver, now called "Wally," was lifted into a tub lined with towels and filled with warm soapy water. Wally's eyes and the inside of his mouth were wiped with a gauze pad. He was given fluids through an IV. To prevent stomach problems in case Wally had swallowed any oil, he was given a dose of antacid. In the tub, Wally was gently rubbed and scrubbed. His fur was stroked in the direction it grew.

It took two people several hours and three washings to remove all the oil. Wally was carefully rinsed, because any soap left in his fur would prevent it from re-waterproofing. Out came the blow-dryer and Wally was puffed and fluffed.

For the next few days, Wally rested and enjoyed a diet of mash fed to him through a water bottle with a long straw. After about a week, Wally was taken to a nearby pond. Oregon school children, who had been following his progress on TV, cheered when they heard that Wally could swim again and would soon be ready to return to his river.

Wally was one of the luckier creatures to be caught in an oil spill. Each year, hundreds of thousands of animals are affected when oil is accidentally released in oceans, lakes, or rivers.

Although new techniques have been used to help these animals recover, many do not survive.

Oil spills occur for a number of reasons. In Wally's case, oil oozed into the river as a result of a break in a pipeline. Some spills occur when tankers break, collide, or run aground. One of America's worst oil spills occurred at Prince William Sound, Alaska, in 1989. The *Exxon Valdez* steered around an iceberg but later struck a jagged reef that ripped a large hole in the ship's metal hull. More than 11 million gallons of greasy black oil poured into the sound. This spill caused an environmental disaster that had long-lasting effects.

When oil is spilled in water, it rises quickly to the surface and spreads out, first into a dark-colored slick, then into a thinner sheen. A sheen glows like the rainbow-colored spot you see when car oil drops on a wet parking lot. Just one tablespoon of oil can form a sheen covering 625 square miles of water. Imagine how far a single gallon can go!

Though it's rare for beavers to be caught in oil spills, other animals often are. Birds are frequent victims. Wildlife veterinarian Scott Newman believes that in the *Exxon Valdez* spill,

Why do you think the author began this story from the perspective of a real beaver who was injured in an oil spill?

A sea otter tries to shake off the oil on the shore of Knights Island after the *Exxon Valdez* oil spill.

Far left: A penguin covered in oil off the coast of South Africa. **Left:** Workers clean oil from the feathers of a duck in Wales.

at least 250,000 birds were killed. It's difficult to know for sure how many birds have died in oil spills because so many drown and sink to the bottom of the ocean. Their feathers, covered in oil, lose their shape and cannot insulate the birds from cold air or water. A spot of oil the size of a quarter can cause a bird to suffer *hypothermia,* a condition in which its body temperature falls too low and the bird cannot survive. When trying to preen, or clean themselves, birds are often poisoned by the oil. They can also be poisoned when they feed on other birds or animals that are covered by oil and have died. Some birds are so shocked, despite being found quickly and carefully washed with toothbrushes and waterpicks, that they die anyway.

How do these photographs of real animals injured in oil spills help the author draw you into her story?

Ducks, loons, eagles, and gulls are among the birds that most frequently suffer "oiling." In June 2000, members of the Oiled Wildlife Care Network rushed off to South Africa to try to save more than 700 penguins when gooey, gunky oil covered the beaches there.

Otters and seals are the victims of oil spills that people usually notice most. Many people think they are cute, so pictures of them covered with gooey oil make headlines around the world. Spills are especially dangerous for otters because they spend most of their time at the water's

surface, where much of the muck is thickest. Rescuing otters is an expensive job. Exxon estimated that they paid $80,000 for each otter they helped following the spill in Alaska.

Oil spills also kill large populations of fish, shellfish, and invertebrates like jellyfish, squid, and octopus. Wild creatures that don't die immediately often die later because their food source or habitat is destroyed. Recently, oily beaches near Miami, Florida, blocked hatching sea turtles from reaching the ocean. A spill off the coast of the Philippines destroyed coral reefs that were home to many marine animals.

The speed with which people respond to an oil spill often determines how many animals are harmed. The more oil that is removed in the first hours and days, the less damage the spill causes. Within minutes of receiving word of a spill, clean-up crews are usually on their way to it. They place long, plastic barriers called "booms," around the spill. These booms look like the plastic lane dividers found floating in a swimming pool. They are like floating fences that stop the flow of oil and keep it from spreading. Next, boats arrive with "skimmers," which are super-sized vacuums. Sometimes materials like straw and sawdust are spread on the surface to soak up the spill. The problem with these materials is that they require so much

Above: A "boom" surrounds the *Exxon Valdez* in an attempt to stop the spilled oil from spreading.

cleanup time. Often, high-pressure hoses are used to wash oil from rocks back into the ocean where it can be picked up by skimmers. Plastic pom-poms, like the ones cheerleaders use, pick up oil from soaked shorelines. Workers also use fertilizers that help oil-loving bacteria grow faster.

In 1990, after the *Exxon Valdez* spill, the U.S. Government passed a law to fight the problem of oil spills. First, a new agency, a.k.a. the Oiled Wildlife Care Network, was set up to ensure quick responses to oil spills. Second, the law requires that all tankers carrying oil must have double hulls by 2010. Also, to prevent future spills, some ships are being designed with alarm systems and automatic shut-down valves. And pipeline workers have begun using x-ray machines that can search for cracks in pipelines, like the one that sent oil spewing into Wally's river home in Oregon.

Unfortunately, there may always be oil spills, but hopefully, they will occur less frequently and cause less damage than they have in the past. ◉

The author uses some abbreviations in the article. How have you figured out what each one stands for?

Stop and Respond

An Important Story

In "After the Spill," the author could have begun her story with some facts and statistics about oil spills. Instead, she describes the people and effort involved in saving Wally, a stranded beaver. How did describing what happened to Wally make the problem of oil spills more real? Discuss your ideas with a partner.

List It!

After you read an informational article like "After the Spill," it helps to look back at the text to make sure you remember the important points. Use the article "After the Spill" to help you write five questions about the effects of an oil spill on the environment. Then ask a classmate to use the article to answer your questions.

Time Line for Disaster

Briefly research major oil spills, beginning with the 1800s. You may use encyclopedias, newspaper articles, or environmental Web sites. Then create a time line of oil spills throughout history.

Got Casein?

You know that milk is good for you, but did you know that milk can also be gooey? Use this recipe made from milk to create your own plastic, ready to be molded into any shape you want!

Follow these simple instructions to make casein (*KAY seen*)—a simple mixture of milk and vinegar—and be amazed at how much fun milk really is!

Gather these items:

- 4 ounces of milk
- 1 teaspoon of vinegar
- a small pan
- a small, clean jar

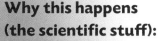

Follow these steps:

1. Heat the milk in a pan until it curdles, or forms lumps. Be sure an adult helps you do this!
2. Slowly and carefully, pour off the runny liquid, keeping the lumps.
3. Put the lumps in the jar and add the vinegar. Let it stand at room temperature for 2 hours.

What will happen:

After an hour or so, you will discover a rubbery blob in the jar! Slowly pour off any runny liquid in the jar. Then experiment with the blob, pulling it into one shape and then another. Once you have a shape you like, let it harden on a paper towel for a few hours. Once it has dried, you can decorate it with acrylic paints, stickers, glitter-glue, or permanent markers.

Why this happens (the scientific stuff):

When milk and vinegar (or any kind of acid) are mixed together, the milk separates into a liquid and a solid made of fat, minerals, and a protein called casein. Casein is made up of very long molecules that bend like rubber until they harden.

LOOKING FOR THE MONSTER

BY ELIZABETH VAN STEENWYK

It was a blustery day in early spring. Although it looked like rain, Jamie couldn't wait to walk down to the lake with his two best friends.

"Guess what!" Jamie called to Alex and Robbie who were walking just ahead of him.

The boys turned around. "What, Jamie?" Robbie asked. "What kind of wild tale do you expect us to believe now?"

Jamie caught up to them. "This isn't a tale at all." He shifted his backpack to his other shoulder. "It's as true and real as the freckles on your face."

"It's real, all right," Alex scoffed. "About as real as you living on another planet."

Jamie ignored him. "I finally saw *it*," he said. His red hair glinted in the sunlight. "I saw the water monster."

Robbie laughed, then said, "Yeah, and I'm a *Tyrannosaurus rex*."

"Just call me Frankenstein," Alex said. "Jamie, everyone knows the stories about a monster being in our lake, but no one has ever seen it."

GUESS WHAT!

"Why do you think you'd be the first one in the world lucky enough to see it?" Robbie asked.

Jamie shrugged. "Because I'm special?"

Robbie and Alex groaned.

Jamie laughed. "OK, OK, I guess I'll have to do better than that."

They neared the corner where they would part to go their separate ways home.

"I'm going out to the lake again after I have a snack," Jamie said. "If you want to see the monster, too, meet me there in half an hour."

"Do you think we're going to fall for that?" Robbie asked.

"I don't think so," said Alex.

"I'll be at the spot where we fished a week ago," Jamie called after them as they walked away. But Robbie and Alex didn't even turn around.

They'll definitely be there, Jamie thought to himself. *They won't be able to help themselves.*

Once inside, Jamie realized that he was as hungry as a bear. He gobbled down two sandwiches before he got his mom's permission to head for the lake. Rain had fallen during the night so there was lots of gooey mud at the lake. But that was to be expected this time of year, so Jamie had put on his boots. And besides, today's plans called for some fancy foot action!

At the lake, Jamie thought about the wet, sticky mud along the shore and how it might add drama to his plan. Jamie had been wanting to play a joke on Robbie and Alex because they never believed anything he said. And his big brother, Cameron, had given him some great ideas. Knowing that Robbie and Alex were as curious as two cats, Jamie and his brother thought up a story just wild enough to get them out here. And the best part was that they would never believe that they could be tricked so easily.

About 20 minutes later, Jamie heard his friends coming, laughing and joking, on the road under the oak trees. Then he heard Robbie say, "He's got as much chance of pulling off some trick on us as my jumping to the moon."

What questions do you have about Jamie's plan?

YOU'RE SO PREDICTABLE!

"Hi, guys," Jamie said as they approached. "I've been waiting for you."

"And we can't wait to see what you've got planned," said Alex.

"We're going to have a tug-of-war," Jamie announced, holding up one end of a long rope.

"Let me guess," Alex said, "we're going to have it with the famous water monster."

"That's right," Jamie replied, acting surprised. "How did you know?"

"You're so predictable," Robbie said. "You know we'd have to pull a monster out of the water to believe it's real."

"Which it isn't," Alex added.

Jamie argued, "Oh, it's real, all right. Here, grab the end of this rope, and I'll show you."

Robbie, Alex, and Jamie held the rope at one end and began to pull. Slowly, the rope came out of the water. The more they pulled, the more rope came out. Then, suddenly, there seemed to be something pulling on the other end!

"Have you got a diver pulling on this rope?" Robbie asked.

"Maybe he's got it fastened to an anchor so we'll think it's the monster pulling back," Alex said, puffing a little as he tugged.

"Guess again," Jamie said.

"I don't need to," Robbie answered, dropping the rope. "The monster on the other end of this rope is like the tooth fairy. It doesn't exist, and your trick isn't working."

The author uses a number of similes—comparisons using the words "like" or "as." How do the story's similes help you visualize the story's setting and action?

Just then, Jamie and Alex felt a tug on the rope that nearly yanked them off their feet and into the mud.

"What was that?" Alex asked, a little worried.

"Pay no attention," Robbie said. "He must have some sort of pulley out there in the water."

"A pulley?" Jamie asked. "How would I connect a pulley to something in the middle of the lake? How would I get out there?"

"Don't play Mr. Innocent with me," Robbie replied. "Maybe your brother helped you figure something out. After all, he's in college now and is taking a lot of science courses."

"But that's the point." Jamie dropped the rope a second so he could wipe his face with his shirtsleeve. "He's *away* at college. How could he help me rig something up when he's 50 miles away?"

Robbie shrugged. "I don't know exactly, but maybe he's using some kind of remote control."

Suddenly, the rope began to move again.

"Look at that!" Alex cried. "Something *is* on the other end! I think I see a *tail!*"

He backed up so fast, he lost his footing and fell in the mud.

"Oh, give me a break, Alex," Robbie said. "There's nothing on the other end of that rope except Jamie's fake monster. Come on, Jamie, show us how you did it so we can go home. It's going to rain any second."

Jamie looked up. The sky *had* clouded over, and the wind began to blow through the treetops. Leaves rustled and the trees shuddered. Waves began to slap at the shore.

"I'm going home," Alex announced and headed for the narrow path through the trees.

"Me, too," Robbie said, following Alex.

"You're just scared," Jamie taunted, "too scared to wait for the monster."

"Cut it out," Robbie yelled. "There *is* no monster."

"Then what is *that?*" Alex quivered, pointing behind them.

Jamie turned around so they wouldn't see him grinning. His brother had shown him how to make the monster's "tail" out of old tires. Last weekend, when no one else was around, Cameron had rigged the tail to thrash in the water when a tug on the rope turned on an underwater engine. How Jamie wished he could tell all this to someone. It was too great to keep to himself.

"Come on, guys, let's really have a tug-of-war now!" Jamie teased as he held out the rope to them.

THEN WHAT IS THAT?

Reluctantly, Robbie and Alex took hold of the rope, and all three of them began to pull. But the force from the other end was so strong, they were nearly dragged into the shallow water.

"I'm out of here!" Alex said. He took one more look at the monster's tail thrashing around in the water, then scrambled up the slippery path as fast as a jackrabbit.

"I'm right behind you, buddy!" Robbie called.

Jamie watched them disappear. He and Cameron would have a great laugh over this. Quickly, he slid the rope into the water. He would have to wait for his brother's help to take apart the gadget.

He hurried home before he got soaked by the rain.

Once Jamie arrived home, he went into the kitchen, where his mother was fixing supper.

"Did you have a good time?" she asked.

"Yeah! I had a great time, Mom," said Jamie.

"By the way, Cameron called from school," Mom said as she took a meat loaf from the oven. "He said to tell you he was sorry about the machine at the lake. He said it doesn't work, and he'll fix it when he comes home tomorrow."

"What?" Jamie was sure he hadn't heard his mother correctly.

"Yes, he said that you'd have to be the monster on your own. What did he mean by *that*?" she asked.

Jamie gulped, his eyes as big as saucers. If Cameron's monster machine wasn't working, then what had been thrashing around in the lake? Was someone playing a trick on *him*? Or, maybe it wasn't a trick at all. Maybe . . . but Jamie didn't dare finish *that* thought. ○

What questions do you have now about what happened at the lake? Why do you think the author decided to end the story in this way?

WHAT?

A PRANK ON THE PRANKSTER?

Were you surprised by the ending of the story, "Looking for the Monster"? Why or why not? What do you think really happened at the end of the story? Write about your ideas in your journal.

AS TALL AS A SKYSCRAPER?

The story "Looking for the Monster" includes many similes—comparisons of two things using the words *like* or *as*. The writer used similes to help create pictures in the readers' minds. Use a sheet of paper to make a two-column chart. In the first column, list four of the similes used in the story. In the second column, draw a picture of the simile and write a sentence to explain what it means.

YOUR OWN PRANKSTER TALE

Do you know anyone like Jamie—someone who likes to play practical jokes? Write a short story about this person. Your story might describe a practical joke this person played on you or one that you played on someone else. Or you could write a fictional story about a prankster. Don't forget to let your reader know whether the story's prankster gets away with the prank or becomes the victim of someone else's prank!

Gooey Rhymes

Poet X. J. Kennedy experiments with words, adds a pinch of humor, and whimsically stirs these gooey rhymes about food. Enjoy your lunch!

No Grosser Grocer

You'll never know a grosser grocer
Than nasty Gnashly Ghastly, no sir!

By cabbages he's long been dreaded.
He chops their heads off, sells 'em shredded.

His margarine is seaweed-green.
Legs poke out of his eggs. Bad scene!

His pecan candies squirm and wiggle.
On jars of pickles, loose lids jiggle.

His coffee cakes look twelve years old.
Nothing he sells has yet been sold.

Except to tribes of mangy trolls—
They like his mildewed jelly rolls!

But if *you* meet this real gross grocer,
Go home and hug your stuffed bear closer.

Italian Noodles

Whenever I
Eat ravioli
I fork it quick
But chew it sloli.

A meatball mound
Of hot spaghetti
Is what I'm rarin' for
Alretti.

Why, when it comes
To pipelike ziti—
Well, I don't know
A sight more priti.

Wouldn't you love
To have lasagna
Any old time
The mood was on ya?

Oh why oh why
Do plates of pasta
Make my heart start
Fluttering fasta?

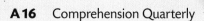

ASKING QUESTIONS

Summer Camp

Authors use many different text features to communicate their ideas. Some authors may use such features as a character's thoughts, journal entries, or letters to show what is going on inside a character's mind, or how the character interacts with others. Careful readers pay attention to these features as they read, and they **ask** themselves **questions** in order to understand their importance to the story.

Tamika is reading a story about a boy who is away at camp for the first time. Most of the story is written in narrative form, but as she reads on, Tamika notices a letter written by the main character. Read the story excerpt below and the questions Tamika asked as she read.

Even though it was only the second day of summer camp, it seemed as if Jake had been there for years. It was bad enough that he didn't have enough spending money, but he couldn't stand his roommate, Neil Parsons. He bragged all the time, he wouldn't give Jake the time of day, and he ate the disgusting camp food. Jake wished his parents had not talked him into going to summer camp. But they really thought they were doing something special for him.

What is this? It looks like a letter. What's a letter doing here? Oh, I see, the author wants me to see what Jake tells his parents.

July 15

Dear Mom and Dad,

Camp is great. We've played some games and told spooky stories around the campfire. The guys in my cabin are all OK. Mom, you were right—the food's OK too, so I won't starve after all. Well, I've got to go. Thanks again for sending me to camp.

Love,

Jake

Hmmm. Jake is not telling his parents the truth. I wonder why? I guess Jake doesn't want his parents to feel bad. Jake must really care about his parents' feelings. I'll bet the author used Jake's letter to show this.

In the next story you read, remember to ask yourself questions like the ones Tamika did. Notice where and how the author uses the characters' journal entries to help you better understand the story and the message the author wants to send.

Surprise Sunday

by June Hetzel

A warm breeze swept through the dining room, providing some relief from the midday heat. Sylvia Delaino bounded down the stairs and picked up her cat, Sylvester, who meowed in protest. "Oh, come on, you lazy old thing! It's a beautiful day outside!" Sylvia drifted out to her father's wheat field and spread out on the blanket she had left there the day before.

"What do you think that cloud looks like, Sylvester?" Sylvia asked aloud. "I think it looks like a horse galloping on the wind. And that one?" she asked, pointing. "Well," she continued, "I think it looks like a knight going into battle."

"I think it looks more like an erupting volcano!" came a voice from somewhere nearby. Sylvia sat up, startled. "Eduardo!" she exclaimed. "Where are you?"

Her brother sat up in the field a few feet away. He parted the wheat stalks with his arms, a huge grin on his face.

"I wish you would stop following me everywhere!" Sylvia said impatiently.

"Hey!" protested Eduardo. "I was here first. Maybe you're following me!"

"And I'm so tired of hearing you talk about that stupid volcano."

"Well, Mount St. Helens is going to erupt someday soon, Sylvia," said Eduardo, excitedly. "You'd better be ready for it!"

"You're making that up!" said Sylvia hotly. "You can have the field to yourself," she huffed, picking up Sylvester. "I'm going home."

Alone in her room, Sylvia took out her diary. She wondered what she would do without this special place to write her thoughts and feelings, especially when her little brother could be so maddening.

May 18
Dear Diary,
    Sometimes Eduardo can be such a pain! All he ever thinks about is that stupid volcano. Sometimes I almost wish it <u>would</u> erupt so he'd stop talking about it!

Mama's voice jolted Sylvia back to reality.
"Sylvia! Time for lunch!"
Sylvia quickly signed her diary entry.

The Exasperated Sylvia Delaino

Then she tucked her diary back into its secret hiding place, safe from her brother's prying eyes. As she walked down the stairs with Sylvester, Sylvia was surprised to hear Mama and Papa talking intently, their voices lowered.

"I still say you spend too much time with Dr. Crandell and Dr. Mullineaux," said Mama. "They are always filling your head with nonsense."

"Norma, they are geologists," insisted Papa. "They know what they are talking about. Mount St. Helens is swelling by 4 to 5 feet every day. The magma is making her bulge. She's going to blow."

Just then Sylvester meowed. Mama and Papa turned to see Sylvia standing at the foot of the stairs, a worried look on her face. Eduardo came strolling in the door at the same moment.

"Good, you're home, Eduardo," said Mama quickly. "Lunch is getting cold."

Papa went outside to help Mama set the table on the porch. As they sat down to eat, Papa noticed a dark cloud in the distance. "Uh-oh," he said. "It looks like rain."

The sky *was* beginning to darken, Sylvia noticed. But it wasn't filled with clouds as it would be if there was going to be rain. Instead, there was only one dark, billowing cloud moving rapidly toward them. Mama said, "We'd better move inside."

As they stood, Sylvia smelled something strong and sour. Almost before she knew what was happening, the dark cloud was upon them, and a veil of darkness had enveloped them.

"Papa!" Sylvia cried. "What's happening?"

"Why is it so dark?" Eduardo wailed.

Then it began to rain. But it wasn't rain. It was light and dry, like floating flakes. They all began coughing.

"Papa, I can't breathe," gasped Sylvia. Her heart pounded.

By now, they were all choking and coughing. There was something wrong with the air—something terribly wrong.

"Quickly, everyone," Mama choked. "Get inside!"

Coughing and gagging, they stumbled inside. Mama rushed to close the windows.

"Henry, what is happening?" cried Mama.

"It's ash. It must be from the volcano," Papa choked out.

Just then, there was a loud rap at the door. It was their neighbor, Mr. Anderson, wearing a mask and holding a radio. "It's Mount St. Helens!" he said, his voice muffled by the mask. "She finally blew!"

"I was right! She blew her top!" Eduardo said, laughing and coughing at the same time. Then, suddenly, he seemed to realize how dangerous the situation was. "It's the end of the world," Eduardo moaned.

Sylvia wanted to hit her brother, but she controlled herself when she saw how pale Eduardo was. She knew then that he was scared, too.

What questions do you have so far about what is happening to the Delaino family?

"This time you might be right, Eduardo," said Sylvia, her voice shaking.

Even Mr. Anderson seemed unsteady. "People are dead. Houses have been destroyed. There was a 5.1 earthquake when she blew. Ash from the eruption is raining down everywhere. It's unbelievable! It's even reaching us here in Yakima, 80 miles away! We should be safe from the lava and the mud, but we may lose our crops."

Papa was stunned. So was Mama.

"I've brought some masks," said Mr. Anderson. "I thought we'd see if anyone needs our help."

"Keep the children inside," Papa told Mama.

Papa and Mr. Anderson put on the masks and went outside. But they soon returned, saying, "There's still too much ash to see anything. We'll wait."

The next day, Papa and Mr. Anderson made it into town. When they returned, Sylvia and Eduardo listened in disbelief to the news they brought. This is unbelievable, Sylvia thought. This couldn't be happening in Yakima. She raced to her room to write in her diary.

May 19th
Dear Diary,

What an incredible two days it has been! When we woke up this morning, it was so eerie to look outside. Everything was covered with gray powder, and it was so quiet. Papa and Mr. Anderson said all of downtown was shut down and dark. But the news from around Mt. St. Helens is even worse. The blast from the volcano and the ash killed everything in its path—birds, fish, insects, trees. Papa says many people were killed, too, but it is too soon to know how many.

Sylvia Delaino

Eduardo, too, was amazed by the news from Mount St. Helens. He wanted to make sure he recorded it all in his scientific journal. After all, scientific history was being made right here in his own hometown!

May 19th

I can't believe everything that's happened. Mount St. Helens finally erupted, just like I said it would. Everywhere Papa and Mr. Anderson went, everything was covered with ash! Papa says the edge of Mount St. Helens collapsed when she blew and shot a bunch of magma into the air. Magma is what you call rocks that are so hot, they melt and turn to lava. Mr. Anderson says that the hot ash from the eruption got all mixed up with snow and ice from the glaciers. Then it oozed down the mountain, picking up everything in its path and making a gooey mess.

Eduardo Delaino's Scientific Journal
Washington State

In fact, each time Papa and Mr. Anderson went out, they found that the eruption had drastically changed their town. Most of the roads had become impassable. Mud had begun flowing down the mountain within minutes of the eruption, and it had laid waste to everything in its path—trees, homes, bridges. Even the

Columbia River was clogged with debris. A large forest directly north of Mount St. Helens had been completely destroyed, and sadly, many people had been killed.

Sylvia recorded it all in her diary.

June 2nd
Dear Diary,
    We have had to stay inside the house for the last two weeks. Papa said until the ash clears from the air, he doesn't want us to go outside. Even the men working in the fields are wearing masks over their faces. They have been trying to remove the ash so we could save some of the wheat crop. But it looks like the wheat crop is lost. Mama says she doesn't know how anything could ever grow again in that gooey mess. At least Eduardo has not been such a pest. When he found out that 57 people had been killed, he finally realized that a volcano erupting is serious business!

Ms. Sylvia Delaino

Why do you think the author used so many of Sylvia's and Eduardo's journal entries in the story?

In fact, Sylvia noticed that Eduardo had been writing in some kind of a diary of his own. *Maybe he was starting to mature a little after all*, she thought.

Meanwhile, Eduardo scribbled furiously in his scientific journal.

June 2nd
    I can't believe the pictures they're showing on TV! Mount St. Helens is 1,300 feet shorter, and the ash has even reached the East Coast!

Eduardo Delaino's Scientific Journal

The days and weeks after the eruption were ones Sylvia would never forget. Her family and the people of Yakima worked tirelessly to clean up the mountains of ash that had covered the town and surrounding farms. Still, she knew that her parents' greatest concern was for their own wheat crop.

June 20th

Dear Diary,

It has been over a month since Mt. St. Helens erupted. Mama is discouraged about the wheat crop. Papa is hopeful, though. He has spent hours talking with a professor who thinks the ash could even help the crops. I don't know about that, but I might even do some soil tests with the ash myself. After all, Eduardo is not the only scientist around here!

Professor Sylvia Delaino

In the first month after the eruption, the north side of Mount St. Helens looked gray and lifeless. The ash that covered everything had turned to goo in the spring's thunderstorms and then had hardened into a dark crust over the landscape. By early summer, however, Papa had heard that signs of life were returning to Mount St. Helens. It looked as if the area around it might recover after all.

Nov. 10th

Dear Diary,

We had a bumper crop this year. Maybe the ash actually did help the soil! In fact, Mama and Papa say this Thanksgiving will be our best one ever. It certainly has been an exciting year for us scientists!

Sylvia Delaino, scientist

Thanksgiving morning dawned clear and bright. In the six months since the eruption of Mount St. Helens, the news for the Delaino family had been better than Mama and Papa could have hoped for. The ash, it turned out, had *not* been toxic, so the family had been in no danger. And while scientists could not definitely say the ash had helped the soil, it certainly had not hurt it, either. And the wheat had grown strong and tall.

Yet when the family gathered around the table for Thanksgiving dinner, Papa was unusually serious. Even Eduardo grew silent.

What changes in the character of Sylvia do you notice through her diary entries? Why do you think the author chose this way to show these changes?

"We have so much to give thanks for this year," said Papa, his voice husky with emotion. "Not only did we bring in a good wheat crop, but we are all here, together, safe and sound."

"Yes, we have much to be thankful for," said Mama, tears in her own eyes.

While they were eating, they talked about the events of the last six months. Now that the eruption of Mount St. Helens—or "Surprise Sunday," as the Delainos had come to call it—was behind them, it seemed that nothing could be better than a day like this.

"Now, if only you two could stop bickering," said Mama.

"Now Mama, we can't expect miracles, can we?" asked Papa, his eyes twinkling.

"Well, I don't know," said Eduardo. "After all, Mount St. Helens made a scientist out of Sylvia. Now, I call *that* a miracle!"

Mama and Papa laughed. And though Sylvia punched her brother in the arm, Eduardo couldn't help but notice that she was laughing, too. ◯

Stop and Respond

Reality Check

"Surprise Sunday" is a fictional story, but Mount St. Helens actually *did* erupt in Washington state in 1980. Writers of realistic fiction often include facts in their stories to make them seem more real. With a group of classmates, gather information about the eruption of Mount St. Helens. Then discuss how well the story reflected the facts.

The Right Perspective?

The characters in "Surprise Sunday" reacted to the eruption of Mount St. Helens in different ways. Get together with two or three of your classmates and discuss their reactions. Whose reaction do you most identify with? Why? Were there any characters whose reactions you found hard to sympathize with or to understand? Why or why not?

Act It Out

What would you do if a volcano erupted 80 miles from your home? Would you pace around, hide under your bed, or try to help others as Mr. Delaino and Mr. Anderson did? How would you find out what was happening at the scene of the disaster? In a small group, create a skit that shows how you might react and what you might do. Each member of your group should take the part of one of the characters. Practice your dialogue and actions, then perform your skit for the rest of the class.

Goo Is a Sticky Subject

by Susan M. Guthrie

Imagine maple syrup oozing onto the top of a tall stack of pancakes. Watch it drip down the sides to make tiny gobs of goo around the bottom. Now imagine a warm piece of crispy toast covered with a glob of gooey honey. Is your mouth watering? Is your stomach growling?

Breakfast wouldn't be the same without these gooey toppings. But where do these thick and sticky sweets come from?

A hike through a hardwood forest can show you the plants and animals responsible for maple syrup, honey, and many other gooey substances. So put on your boots, since it can get damp in the woods, and **let's go!**

A black and orange monarch butterfly flutters past. It heads straight for a field of wildflowers by the trail that leads into the forest. Let's follow it!

Monarch butterflies drink the nectar from a variety of flowers but lay their eggs only on the stems and leaves of the milkweed plant. When the eggs hatch, the tiny larvae begin chomping the leaves of the plant. The milky white goo inside the leaves and stems contains small amounts of a rubbery substance. It can be poisonous to most animals but not to the monarch. The monarch larvae absorb it into their bodies. Predators, seeing the bright colors of the monarch larvae and butterfly, remember their foul taste and avoid them.

There are other types of insects that can be found on milkweed plants. How do they adapt to this poisonous goo?

Great numbers of yellow aphids can be found clinging to the stems of milkweed plants. They suck the juice from the plant for food. And where there are aphids, there are often ants. The ants watch over the aphids, much as a rancher watches over a herd of cows. Why? The ants come to feed but not on the milkweed plant. When an ant strokes an aphid with its antennas, the aphid releases a tiny drop of honeydew that the ant eats. Honeydew goo is made up of partially-digested plant sap and other wastes. But *you* might want to stick with maple syrup and honey!

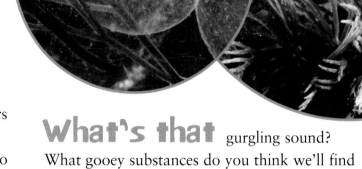

Baby blobs! These frog eggs are covered in a gooey mass to protect the developing embryo inside.

Speaking of honey,

what's that buzzing sound? It looks like there are some honeybees buzzing around the flowers of the sage plants that are growing next to the milkweed. One of the bees has disappeared into the forest. Since bees, like butterflies, drink the sweet and sticky nectar of flowering plants, maybe it will lead us to more flowers. Or maybe it will lead us to its gooey "home base." Let's follow the bee and find out!

The forest seems dark at first. Once our eyes adjust to the shadows, however, we see snails crawling on damp leaves near a fallen maple tree. Snails, like insects, are invertebrates. But snails don't have legs—they move along on one long muscular "foot." To help them move, they produce a sticky goo to glide on. Maybe that's why snails move so slowly. It's like waiting for little bits of sidewalk to extend out in front of you, inch by inch. It's probably a good thing people don't need goo to move!

A jay just dipped low overhead while going deeper into the woods. It's time for us to move on, too!

What's that gurgling sound?

What gooey substances do you think we'll find near the water?

Amphibians lay their eggs in or near slow-moving fresh water. Each egg is covered with a jellylike goo. A common toad can lay as many as 6,000 eggs at one time in two long strands of jelly. Frogs, too, lay their eggs in a gooey mass. The jelly protects each developing embryo from the outside world.

> What questions do you still have about how honey and maple syrup are made?

Next to the base of a tree and near the

water is the shell of a bird's egg. Maybe it's from the nest of the jay we saw earlier.

Birds' eggs have several kinds of sticky goo inside. A clear whitish substance surrounds and protects the yolk where the embryo grows, much like the gooey material around amphibian embryos. This whitish goo is made up of four layers, with the thickest layer next to

the yolk. This part also has two spiral bands—the chalazae *(kuh LAY zuh)*—that are attached to opposite ends of the yolk. These bands, or cords, hold the yolk in place inside the shell.

People have found many uses for the gooey insides of birds' eggs, especially chickens' eggs. Fried or scrambled, eggs can be a delicious addition to a breakfast of pancakes or honey toast. They are also a key ingredient in cookies and cakes. Artists have mixed egg yolks with pigment since ancient times to make a special kind of paint called "egg tempera."

Look ahead! There are bees zipping in and out of the white bee boxes under that large sugar maple tree. Have we finally found the source of maple syrup? Does it come from those boxes?

Maple syrup is a sweet, gooey substance that comes from the sap of sugar maple trees. In early spring, when the sap begins to rise from the trees' roots to their leaf buds, people drill holes into the trees. Tubes, or spouts, are placed into the holes to collect the sap. The maple sap looks watery and colorless at first. But when it is boiled, the water in the liquid evaporates and it turns a golden brown color, becoming thick and sticky.

No one knows how long people have been collecting sap from sugar maple trees and making syrup. We do know that Native Americans who once lived near the Great Lakes and the St. Lawrence River made maple syrup long before European explorers came to North America.

Maple syrup is a kind of goo that comes from plant sap. Does honey ooze from a plant, too?

Drip drop . . . These buckets help collect sap from the trees.

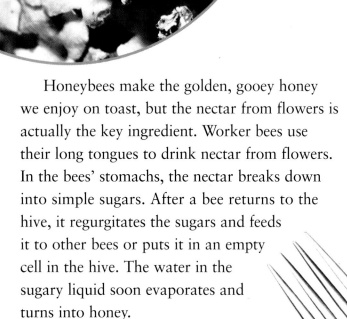

Busy Bees Talk about sticking to your work! In the U.S. alone, bees produce about 200 million pounds of honey.

Honeybees make the golden, gooey honey we enjoy on toast, but the nectar from flowers is actually the key ingredient. Worker bees use their long tongues to drink nectar from flowers. In the bees' stomachs, the nectar breaks down into simple sugars. After a bee returns to the hive, it regurgitates the sugars and feeds it to other bees or puts it in an empty cell in the hive. The water in the sugary liquid soon evaporates and turns into honey.

People have been collecting and eating honey since the Stone Age. Some prehistoric people might even have made "hives" from hollow logs, pots placed on their sides, or upside-down baskets. Later, people developed better ways to attract bees. Colonists may have brought honeybees to North America from England as early as 1622.

We have come to the end of our walk in the forest.

We have learned where maple syrup, honey, and other sticky, gooey substances come from. Is that your stomach rumbling? Then let's hike home quickly and have something deliciously gooey to eat! ○

Why do you think the author used a hike in the woods to present the information in this article?

Goo or Goodie?

Gooey things can be delicious, like blueberry pie or an extra-chewy brownie, or not so appetizing, like thick, smelly tar or snail slime. It all depends on your point of view! Think of a gooey substance that you love to eat or one that causes you to lose your appetite. Write a paragraph that persuades a reader to feel the opposite way about it than you do. Try to appeal to your readers' sense of taste, touch, sight, smell, and sound. Share your description with a few classmates and watch their reactions.

Art That Drips, Squishes, and Oozes

Grab your scissors and some old magazines and start collecting pictures of gooey things! Food magazines are good for gooey chocolate or syrupy desserts, while science magazines are great for photos of shiny oil slicks, sticky maple sap, or glowing lava. Once you have a good collection of images, arrange them into a collage on posterboard. Then write some "goo-ily" descriptive words to go with your pictures.

Goo Galore!

Poets carefully choose each word in a poem to create pictures in their readers' minds. And what could be a better subject for a poem than something truly gooey, like honey, maple syrup, or hot fudge? Write a poem describing a gooey substance of your choice. Make sure to use precise verbs and adjectives to create vivid images for your readers.

Let's Write

Cookbook of Gooey Goodies

Some of the most delicious treats are made with gooey chocolate, honey, or cheese. Just imagine, for example, a pizza oozing with delicious sauce and covered with gobs of gooey cheese. With two classmates, create a Cookbook of Gooey Goodies. Gather recipes from family members, friends, or cookbooks. Try to include at least one recipe for breakfast, lunch, dinner, dessert, a snack, and a drink. Create an illustration of a particularly gooey goodie for your cover.

Gallery of Goop

Think of a gooey substance that you've read about in this issue, such as honey, tar, volcanic lava, or frog jelly. Do some research about how the substance is made, what it is made of (the physical properties that make the substance gooey), what the substance is used for, and how it affects other creatures. Create a fact sheet with five of the most interesting things you learned. Design the title so that it illustrates the substance's properties.

A Monster of a Tale

In an old horror movie called *The Blob,* a gooey, shapeless monster terrorizes a town. Invent your own monster that either comes out of something gooey, produces a slimy substance, or is made of goo itself. Write a story about the monster and what happens to it. Illustrate your story with vivid pictures.

More Books

Arnold, Nick. *Blood, Bones, and Body Bits.* Scholastic Paperbacks, 1998.

Branzi, Sylvia. *Hands-On Grossology: The Science of Really Gross Experiments.* Planet Dexter, 1999.

Kerrod, Robin. *All About Volcanoes.* Lorenz Books, 2000.

On the Web

How to Make Slime
http://www.fatlion.com/science/slime.html

A Lesson on Making Maple Syrup
http://www.spruceharbor.com/commun~1/kitchen/maple.htm

Recipes for Making Slime
http://freeweb.pdq.net/headstrong/slime.htm

Across the Curriculum

Science

You can find out what happens to oil after a spill. All you need is a large, clear glass bowl and some vegetable oil. If you want, add a little cocoa powder to the oil to see it better. Fill the bowl three-fourths full with water and place it on a table. Pour a little oil on the water and watch what happens. Does the oil mix with the water or does it stay on top? Why do you think wind, currents, and tides are important in predicting where oil might go after a spill? Share your ideas with the class.

Science/Social Studies

The La Brea tar pits are pools of pitch (tar) that bubble up from large oil deposits under the city of Los Angeles, California. About 10,000 to 40,000 years ago, saber-toothed tigers, giant ground sloths, mammoths, insects, and plants fell into the tar and have been preserved in near-perfect condition. Today, the La Brea tar pits are a popular tourist attraction. Find out more about the tar pits—when they were discovered and how scientists have worked to study and preserve them. Then present your information to the class.

Make Your Own
"VOLCANO SURPRISE"

If you were fascinated by the facts about volcanoes in "Surprise Sunday," you'll love making your own erupting volcano. This project is guaranteed to make a mess, so you might want to do it outside!

What you'll need:

- A sturdy sheet of plywood (this will be the base for your volcano)
- Modeling clay (plasticine)
- 1 tbsp. of baking soda
- 1 tbsp. of liquid dish soap
- $\frac{1}{4}$ cup of vinegar
- Red and yellow food coloring
- Your parents' permission!

What to do:

1. Form a cone shape with the modeling clay. Work the clay until you get a shape you like. It is a good idea to leave some cracks and crevices for the "lava" to flow down.
2. Use your fingers to create a hole in the center of the cone.
3. Once the volcano is firmly set, put the baking soda, dish soap, and some food coloring into the hole.
4. When you're ready for your "surprise," add the vinegar. Stand back, and watch your volcano erupt!

If the lava flow seems a little thick, the next time, add a little water in the hole before you add the vinegar.

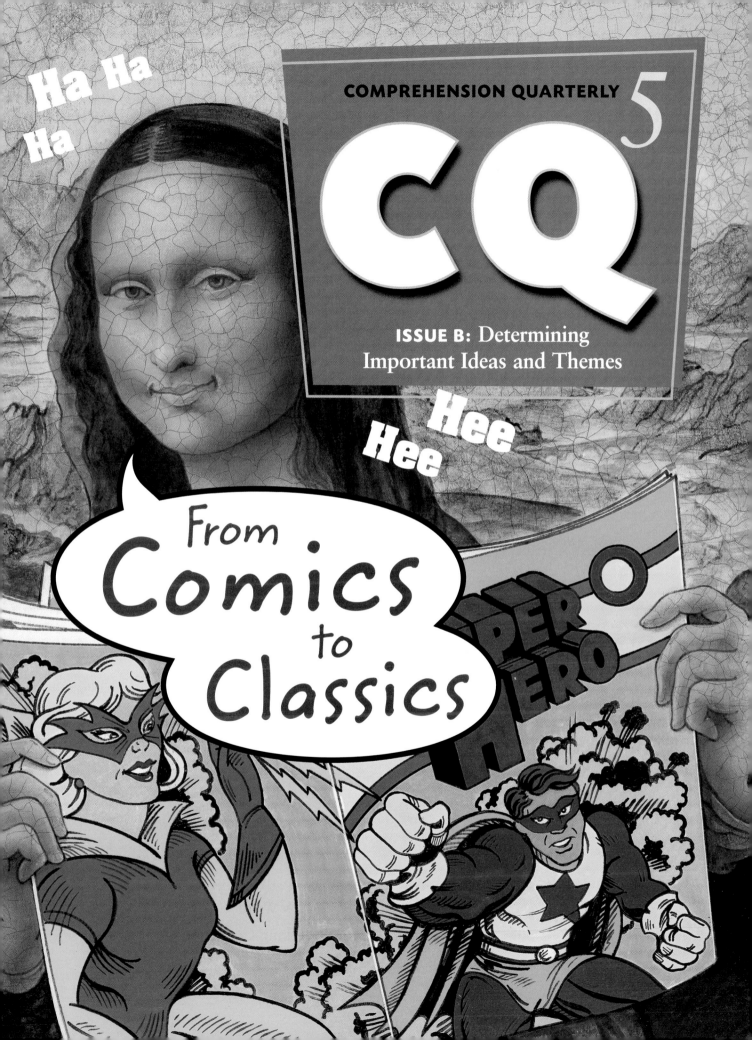

From Comics to Classics

THINK ABOUT: Determining Important Ideas and Themes

B4

B19

B25

In this issue:

DETERMINING IMPORTANT IDEAS AND THEMES

The Moral of the Story

Yolanda picked up the book of Aesop's fables and thumbed through it to find the story about the fox and the grapes. The first time Yolanda had read the fable, she had read it just for fun. But now Yolanda had an assignment. She was supposed to write about a time when the moral of the fable had applied to her own life. So she wanted to read "The Fox and the Grapes" again. This time, she would think more carefully about the moral and what it meant.

The Fox and the Grapes

One hot day, a fox spied a lovely bunch of grapes. They hung overhead on a vine that grew in a tree.

"Just the thing to quench my thirst," said the fox. He jumped as high as he could, but it was not high enough.

Again the fox tried, and again he missed. He kept on jumping—three, four, five times more.

At last the fox gave up. He stuck his nose in the air and left, saying, "I'm sure those grapes are sour."

Moral: It is easy to dislike what you cannot have.

I see! It's like when Amy didn't invite me to her party. I said I didn't care because I hated slumber parties. But I really wanted to go.

Yolanda's purpose for reading had changed. So what she thought was important in the story changed, too. The first time, she read just to get an idea of what was happening. The second time, she read to **determine how the important ideas and themes** in the story related to her own life.

Think about something you have read recently and your purpose for reading it. Now imagine another reason for reading. Perhaps you want to retell the story to a younger child. Or maybe you just found out there's going to be a test on the material. How does your new purpose change your thoughts about what is important in the text?

The Giant's Beanstalk

by Peg Hall

Once upon a time, a giant lived in a castle high in the clouds. Julius wasn't your average giant. He liked to read and gaze at the stars and think deep thoughts. But most of all, he liked to garden.

One fine day, Julius hummed as he pulled weeds. He smiled at the sight of a perfect rose. But he stopped short when he saw the beanstalk he had planted just that morning.

"Goodness!" said Julius. "That's growing fast! Even for a gardener with a green thumb!"

The beanstalk covered the east end of his garden. It wound around trees and over two birdbaths before climbing the wall and disappearing.

Julius tugged. "Seems plenty strong," he said. "I wonder where it goes." Still grasping the beanstalk, he stepped over the wall and into a sea of clouds.

For what seemed like hours, Julius climbed down the long, twisting stalk. At last he felt solid earth beneath his feet. The clouds dissolved to reveal a wide, green valley. In the distance, a ribbon of silver wound its way past a small village.

Stop for a moment and think about your purpose for reading. What do you want to know?

"That looks interesting," said Julius. Ten great steps took him to the village. The streets were a beehive of activity—until someone screamed.

"Giant! Run for your lives!"

People darted off. Horses galloped away. Doors slammed. In seconds, the streets were deserted.

"I'm not that kind of giant," muttered Julius sadly, but no one was around to hear.

Or almost no one. There was a sniff. Then a sob. Julius followed the sounds. Behind a mountain of hay, he found a young girl.

"What's the matter?" asked Julius, bending closer.

The girl wiped tear-stained cheeks. "Oh, go ahead," she said. "I may as well be eaten by an ugly giant as starve to death."

"I wouldn't eat you!" Julius protested. Then he asked, "Am I really so ugly?"

The girl studied Julius before replying. "No, but you *are* a giant. And everyone knows that giants eat people and grind their bones to make bread."

"*I* don't," said Julius. "Now, what's your name—and why are you crying?"

"I'm Meg," she sighed. "And I'm crying because I'm hungry."

"Why not eat something?" suggested Julius.

"There's nothing *to* eat," said Meg. "We're *all* hungry."

Julius stood up and looked around at the green fields surrounding the village. He realized that there was nothing to eat growing there. The fields were a sea of weeds.

"Why hasn't anyone planted beans and corn and wheat?"

"Because the fields belong to Jack," said Meg. "And he won't plant anything. All we eat is what we find in the forest. At least, that's how things are now."

"How were things before?"

"We owned the land. We grew things to eat and sold what was left. Everyone had enough."

"What happened?" asked Julius.

"Jack wanted everything. He bought all the land. If someone wouldn't sell, awful things happened. Soon he owned everything, but he let the fields turn to weeds. People bought food with the gold he gave them— until it was gone."

"Maybe I can help," said Julius. "Where can I find this fellow?"

"That way," said Meg.

Julius headed off. Twenty steps later, he reached a huge, stone house. He leaned over and knocked on the great door: Bam! Bam!

A man yanked the door open and stared up at Julius. He clutched a half-eaten turkey drumstick in one hand.

"Are you Jack?" asked Julius politely.

"Maybe," said Jack. "Who's asking?"

"I'm Julius. We need to talk."

"Nobody's home," said Jack. "Come back later!" He slammed the door.

Julius was bewildered. He *knew* someone was home. And he knew it had to be Jack. So he knocked again: BAM! BAM!

> What important characteristics have you learned about Jack and the giant so far?

"Get lost!" shouted Jack.

Julius scratched his head. Maybe he'd try later. Then he saw some tall trees nearby. "I'll just hang around," he said, "and see what I can see."

So Julius hid behind the tallest, thickest tree. For a long time, nothing happened. Then he heard a honkety-honk.

Julius peered through a second-floor window. Jack was opening a cage. A cloud of white feathers shot out and a beautiful goose flew around the room. It landed on a stool.

"Lay, goose, lay!" commanded Jack.

There was another honkety-honk. A moment later, a gleaming egg appeared under the goose.

"Pure gold, as usual," said Jack. Then he stuffed the goose back into its cage and left.

"A goose that lays golden eggs!" said Julius. "So *that's* Jack's secret!"

Julius *had* to get hold of that goose. "It'll help the villagers," he said. "And since Jack is so greedy, he would never think to share."

Just then the front door slammed, and Jack came out, whistling. Soon he was out of sight.

Julius lost no time. He stuck one arm in the window and felt around for the cage. Then he pulled it out, knocking several stones off around the window in the process.

Back at the village, people were waiting. They looked nervous at the sight of Julius, but no one screamed.

"I told them you'd help," said Meg.

"I don't see how," said a beanpole of a man.

"And we don't need another mouth to feed. Especially one that big."

"You won't need to feed me," said Julius. "Look!"

He took the goose from the cage and sat it on a wooden bench. "Lay, goose, lay!" he said. "Please."

The villagers gasped at the sight of a golden egg. "It's for you," Julius told Meg.

After that, everything changed. Each day the goose presented Julius with another golden egg. He used the first week's worth to buy the land back from Jack. The greedy fellow was glad to have the gold as he knew he'd never get the goose back. He left his huge house and took off for parts unknown.

Julius had Meg help him distribute the eggs fairly. Soon everyone had fine clothes and delicious food, and no one had to work. Julius made himself a cozy home in a huge, old barn. And everyone prepared to live happily ever after.

However, that's not what happened. People ate too much and spent long hours staring into space. They worried about dressing better than their neighbors. And with nothing else to do, they started to argue.

Meg complained to Julius, "No one gets along anymore. All they care about is their next golden egg."

> The typical fairy tale would end here. Why do you think the author is continuing the story?

Julius looked up from the radishes he was planting. He had started a garden to give himself something to do.

"Maybe I shouldn't have kept the goose," he said. "Maybe I should just have taken a few eggs. After all, it's not like anyone *needs* so much gold."

"You're right," sighed Meg.

"Honk!" said the goose, flying up on Julius' shoulder. "Why didn't you just say so? Honkety-honk!"

Meg and Julius were stunned. "You can talk?" asked Meg.

"If I want to," replied the goose. "But that's not important. What *is* important is that you don't want all these golden eggs around. And frankly, I don't want to lay them."

"I'm sorry," said Julius. "I never thought to ask you how you felt about it."

"What *do* you want?" asked Meg.

"I want to be a normal goose—laying normal eggs and raising normal goslings."

"Then that's how it's going to be," promised Julius.

Later, a woman came to get an egg. "The goose is done laying golden eggs," said Julius.

"DONE?" screeched the woman. "What do you mean, *done?*"

It didn't take long for word to spread. Soon an army of angry villagers marched toward the barn.

"What are we supposed to do?" a man shouted. "Sure, we can eat the goose. But then what? We'll starve!"

"Nobody's going to be eating *this* goose," said Julius. "Besides, why will you starve?"

"We won't have money for food, you fool," said a woman.

"You have your land," said Julius.

"We can *grow* food," added Meg, "like we used to."

"What? Work from dawn to dusk again?" shouted someone. "Why should we?"

"Because we were happy when we did," Meg said softly.

"Happy?" A long silence followed.

At last an old woman stepped forward. "Meg's right," she said. "We worked hard, but we were happy."

Low murmurs ran through the crowd, and several people nodded.

"I'll help," Julius offered. "I have lots of plants started here."

Soon the fields were green with beans and corn and wheat. Every day, the villagers planted and weeded and picked their crops. Every night, they went to bed with full bellies and light hearts.

As for Julius, he never returned to his lonely castle in the clouds. He liked living close to Meg—and to the goose and her noisy goslings.

The villagers were happy to have a friendly giant around. Especially since Julius' green thumb meant things would always grow—as long as everyone worked hard.

And that was fine. As Julius said to Meg, "The easiest things aren't necessarily the best." ○

Now that you've finished the story, what do you think the author's purpose was for continuing it?

Stop and Respond

Purpose for Reading

Think about your purpose for reading the story, "The Giant's Beanstalk." Did you want to read it to make comparisons to "Jack and the Beanstalk," just for fun, or for some other reason? How did your purpose help you decide what was important in the story? Discuss your ideas with a partner.

Making Comparisons

How are the characters of Jack and the giant in this story like those in the classic tale, "Jack and the Beanstalk"? How are they different? Create a Venn diagram to compare one of the characters as he appears in both stories.

THE GIANT

The Giant's Beanstalk   Jack and the Beanstalk

- friendly
- gentle
- likes to garden

- huge
- lives in clouds

- mean
- eats people

Things That Matter

Record a sentence or two from the story that tells what *you* think is an important idea. Remember that different people consider different things as important in their lives. Write a list of three things that you think each of the following characters would consider important:

- **Julius**
- **Meg**
- **Jack**

Now write a list of three things *you* consider important.

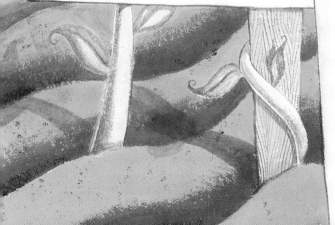

Nursery Rhymes: Not Really for Kids?

Most of the classic nursery rhymes you learned as a small child have been around for hundreds of years. However, if what some people say about their origins is true, they certainly weren't created with children in mind. Can you match each description to a nursery rhyme?

1. The title of this rhyme is the name given to an English cannon. When the cannon was hit by enemy fire, it fell and broke.

2. Some say this rhyme is about a disease that killed thousands of people. Their bodies were often burned to ashes.

3. This rhyme may tell about medieval taxes. One-third of what a person produced went to the king. Another third went to the nobles. The person got to keep what was left.

4. An old custom for greeting the new year was to jump over a candle. If the flame didn't go out, the jumper would have good luck.

5. Some say this rhyme talks about a king who is away. People thought he should be home, taking care of his country.

> Baa, baa, black sheep, have you any wool?
> Yes sir, yes sir, three bags full.
> One for my master,
> One for my dame,
> And one for the little boy who lives down the lane.

> Humpty Dumpty sat on a wall.
> Humpty Dumpty had a great fall.
> All the king's horses and all the king's men
> Couldn't put Humpty together again!

> Jack be nimble,
> Jack be quick.
> Jack jump over the candlestick!

> Ring around the rosie,
> A pocket full of posies,
> Ashes, ashes!
> We all fall down.

> Little boy blue, come blow your horn.
> The sheep's in the meadow; the cow's in the corn.
> And where is the little boy who looks after the sheep?
> Under the haystack, fast asleep.

The Finest Present

by David R. Collins

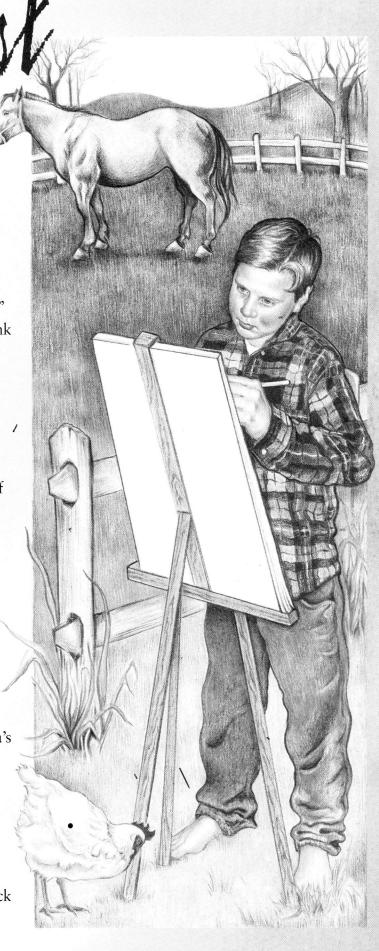

"Get away from here, you little pest! Shoo!"

"How's the picture coming along, boy? Think you can finish it before the holidays?"

"Sure hope so, Doc. I'd work a lot faster if this silly rooster of mine would stop pecking at my drawing stand."

"Maybe he thinks he's a woodpecker," the old man laughed back. "Let's take a rest for a minute. This horse of mine doesn't get tired of standing up, but I sure do."

"Ma fixed us a special batch of lemonade. I'll go get it."

As the slim, barefooted boy scampered across the barnyard, ducks, chickens, and two spotted cats dashed out of his way. The old man sat down on the back porch. In a few moments the boy came out carrying two tall glasses of lemonade.

"This'll make you feel sassy," the boy beamed. "That's what Pa always says about Ma's lemonade since she makes it so sour."

"Well, I think this lemonade has a fine taste to it."

The boy and the man sat and drank their lemonade.

"I have never seen such a warm November here in Missouri," Doc said. "There's not a speck of snow yet."

"I'm glad there hasn't been any. Gives me more time to draw outside."

"You sure do like to draw, don't you? Well, I think it's a fine way for a young boy to keep out of mischief. Yes, we're all glad that you moved out here from Chicago. Your pa's a fine contractor; he builds a good, sturdy building. And your ma, she makes awful sassy lemonade."

"Want some more?"

"No, let's get the picture done. Mrs. Sherwood would love to see that picture. She hasn't been feeling too well lately, but I think seeing that horse sketched out—well, that might be just the medicine she needs. She loves that animal as much as I do."

The boy worked faster now. Time was running out. The winter snowstorms would soon arrive. Often the snow made prisoners of the farmers, shutting them off from the rest of the world.

"I'll be headed home now," the old man said. "The sun's almost gone, anyway."

"OK, Doc. I think one more session will do it." The boy nodded. "I just have to finish a few more shadows and do the horse's eyes."

"Glad to hear it, boy. Thank your ma for the tasty lemonade. See you tomorrow."

What important things do you know about the boy and the man from their dialogue?

But the mild days had run out. During the night, a freezing rain smothered the countryside. On top of that came giant drifts of snow. Days became weeks as the boy waited impatiently for a warm sun to thaw the frozen earth. But the thaw didn't come. As the holidays approached, the boy grew more and more worried. He begged his parents to let him go to Doc's farmhouse. "He wants the drawing for a present for his wife because he thinks it might make her feel better. I would just need one session."

"We can't let you go," his mother answered. "Some of these drifts are over your head."

Sadly the boy returned to his room, gazing hopelessly at the unfinished sketch.

It wasn't until a week before Christmas that the snow began to melt. By Christmas Eve, much of the snow had melted, but a bitter wind blew fiercely against the farmhouse.

"Let me try to make it to Doc's house," the boy begged. "I have to finish the picture for Doc. He's got to have it tomorrow."

"But this wind will blow you away," his mother argued.

"Please may I try?"

The boy's father and mother looked at each other. "Well, go ahead, but bundle up," the boy's father finally nodded, "and if the wind is too fierce . . ."

"I'll come back if I can't get through. I promise."

Quickly the boy hurried to his room and put on his heaviest clothes. With great care, he wrapped the picture and put his best sketching pencils in a wooden box. Bravely he plunged out into the driving wind.

Flakes of snow stung his skin as the boy crossed the barnyard. His eyes watered and his feet could scarcely be pulled from the ground. He paused for a moment against the barn, regripped his picture and box of pencils, and started again. He had only gone a few steps when a violent gust of wind grabbed his box of pencils and hurled them through the air. Another gust of air threw him back against the side of the barn. He remembered his promise. Sadly, he stumbled back to the farmhouse.

That evening was a happy time for the rest of the family. They sang, popped corn, and played games. The boy tried to be happy, but he could not forget the drawing.

Sensing their son's disappointment, his mother and father tried to cheer him up. "You mustn't be this unhappy. Doc Sherwood will understand."

"But I only had the eyes of the horse and a few shadows left. Just one more day and I would have finished."

"Couldn't you add those things with what you remember?" his father asked.

In his mind, the boy tried to recall the scene. "I don't know if I could or not."

"You won't know unless you try," his father suggested.

Eagerly, the boy ran to his room and took out the picture. He closed his eyes and tried to recreate the horse standing before him. Digging a lone sketching pencil from beneath his bed, he slowly added the shadows to the picture. "But how did the eyes look?" he wondered. He just couldn't remember. Finally, he put his pencil down and joined the rest of the family.

"It's no use," he said. "I just have to see those eyes to be able to draw them."

"Well, why can't you make the eyes of the horse as you think Doc would *like* them to be? You want the picture to make him happy and please his wife. You make happy eyes on so many of the animals you draw. Draw these eyes the way you feel they *should* be," his mother replied.

When you draw, do you use your imagination to fill things in?

The boy thought about what his mother had said. He remembered all the wonderful afternoons with Doc—all the laughter. Even the horse seemed to be laughing with them. Slowly the boy began sketching. Finally, he put his pencil down and crawled into bed.

A warm sunrise greeted the family the next morning. By midafternoon, the wind had died and the snow was fast turning into giant puddles. The boy wrapped his picture and made his way down the muddy road to Doc's farmhouse.

"Why, bless my soul!" the old man shouted. "Martha, we have company." He helped the boy with his boots and coat. A small woman with a dark blue shawl welcomed him into the parlor.

"Sorry we had to postpone our sessions," Doc Sherwood smiled. "And you were just about done with the picture."

"Well, I . . . I wanted to . . . to finish it myself—so you would have it today," the boy stammered. "I tried to remember the eyes as best as I could. Ma said to sketch them the way I felt them. You . . . you probably won't like the picture, but I brought it anyway."

"Well, by all means, let's see it," Doc grinned.

As the boy unwrapped the picture, his face felt hot. He had a sudden urge to run from the room. But it was too late.

He faced his picture, then turned it around so Doc and his wife could see. For several moments, there was no sound in the room. The boy stared blankly at the back of the picture, unable to face his hosts.

"I . . . I can try again. I shouldn't have tried to . . ."

The boy stopped as he noticed the tears in Mrs. Sherwood's eyes.

"It's so beautiful, so beautiful," Mrs. Sherwood murmured. "How could such a small boy do something so perfect?"

"It's the finest picture I've ever seen," Doc Sherwood announced. "And the finest present we could have had."

"You really think it's all right?" the boy questioned. "You think the eyes are all right?"

"Oh, the eyes are so warm, so happy," Mrs. Sherwood smiled.

"Yes, you've done yourself proud, boy," Doc Sherwood exclaimed, as he took the picture and placed it over the fireplace mantel. "But say, you forgot something here."

"I . . . I did?"

"I'm no artist, but I know one thing. An artist signs his own work."

"But I . . . I'm no artist," the boy shook his head.

"Oh, yes," Mrs. Sherwood said softly. "You're an artist with your hands, and more important, with your heart."

The boy knew he couldn't refuse. With a trembling hand, he printed his name.

Walt Disney ⦿

Why was it important for the author not to use the boy's name throughout the story?

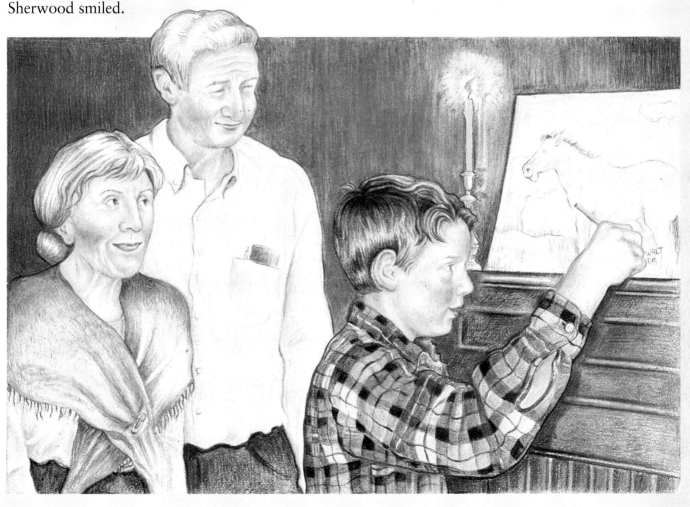

Changing Purposes

Think back to when you read the title, "The Finest Present." Perhaps you wanted to find out what the present was and what made it the "finest." Once you started to read the story, did your purpose for reading change? Maybe you wanted to know if the picture would be finished in time. Explain your thoughts in a short paragraph.

Get the Picture?

Figures of speech don't always mean exactly what the words say! Look back through the story for examples, such as "the snow made prisoners of the farmers" and "a freezing rain smothered the countryside." Think about what the words in the phrase actually say. Then think about what the figure of speech means. Draw two pictures—one that shows each meaning.

So Many Choices

Walt Disney created many characters who have become classics. Think about the movies, cartoons, and stories you have seen or read. List three of your favorite characters. Then take a survey with the class and make a list of your class's top three favorites.

Cartoon Art

The key to cartooning is keeping it simple. Start by drawing some cartoon faces. Here are some helpful hints.

1 **Start** with a row of circles and ovals.

2 **Add eyes** to each face. Make the eyes show what your cartoon character is thinking or feeling.

3 **Add a nose** to each.

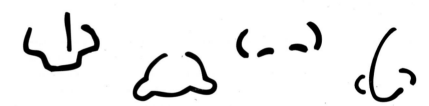

4 **Add a mouth.** Remember that the mouth, too, shows what your character is thinking or feeling.

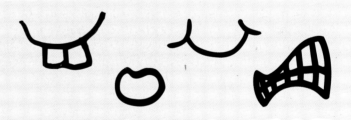

5 **Now add some ears.**

6 **Finish** the face off with some hair —unless you want a bald character!

DETERMINING IMPORTANT IDEAS AND THEMES

Looking Bold

Nate took his social studies book out of his backpack and stared at it. He had an entire chapter to read before he could go outside. And he had to read it carefully because Mr. Sorvino was giving a quiz. Nate was sure there would be no baseball for him today.

The chapter was 12 pages long, packed full of words. He'd never get through it! But then Nate remembered what Mr. Sorvino had told the class. "Skim through a chapter before you start reading," he'd said. "Look for clues as to what is important. That will help you know where to concentrate your time as you read."

Nate shrugged. It was worth a try. He slowly turned the pages. First his eyes went to the photos and their captions. That was all probably important information. After all, if it wasn't, they wouldn't have wasted the space.

Next, Nate looked at the words. The headings jumped out at him right away— big and bold and hard to miss. They were all questions, he noted. Some boldfaced words stood out, too. He remembered that those words could be found in the glossary at the back of the book. And there, on page 202, was a chart titled "Things to Remember." That *had* to be important.

As Nate started reading, he thought about the headings, looking for information that answered the question each one asked. He paid special attention to the boldfaced words. He even checked the glossary when he didn't understand one of the words.

Twenty minutes later, Nate was done. As he closed the book, he realized that his homework assignment hadn't been bad at all. And he was pretty sure he knew what important things Mr. Sorvino would ask about in the quiz.

Grabbing his baseball mitt, Nate ran outside. It was time to play ball!

Think about reading one of your textbooks. What features help you **determine the important ideas** in the book? How are the chapters arranged? Are there pictures? charts? graphs? Are some words italicized or boldfaced? If so, what does that mean? All of these text features are clues to what is important. Be sure to use them to help you as you read!

Willa S. Speare, Star Woes

by Charles Hirsch

Some kids dream of creating the coolest site on the Internet. Others want to become superstar athletes, but I, Willa S. Speare, I dream of a life on the stage. That's why I went to Camp King Lear last summer and am here again this summer. But this morning, after my audition piece, that dream seemed to walk right out the theater door.

Act 1
Scene 1

Act 1

Scene 2

Ms. Windsor, the director

Which character shouldst thou play?

Lady Macbeth

Juliet

Romeo

Puck

Ms. Windsor, the camp director, was smiling broadly after my audition. Was she trying to keep from laughing? Then she said, "Your work was so totally unique—so totally *you*, Willa."

What was *that* supposed to mean? I wondered. *Oh, so totally, me?* How about so totally dumb? So totally embarrassing? And so totally in front of you, Ms. Windsor, the person I so totally(!) wanted to impress more than anyone in the world? I knew I had made the biggest blunder of my brief life. I wanted to hide. I'd never get one of the lead roles at this year's camp show. I had to explain what had happened, but I had to wait until *all* the auditions were over. Finally, Ms. Windsor came out of the theater. I leaped forward.

"Ever since I first met you at camp last summer, I couldn't wait until we—me, you, and Will, as I refer to William Shakespeare—would be reunited this year. But woe is me, Ms. Windsor," I began. "I have to explain what happened this morning."

I set the stage, lifting my words from Shakespeare himself. "All the world's a stage, and all the kids at Camp King Lear merely players. We make our exits and our entrances. But somewhere I made a wrong turn."

Ms. Windsor seemed intrigued. I was gathering steam. I was on a roll. So I seized the moment and continued.

"Before I came to camp this summer, I lived, ate, and dreamed Shakespeare, 24-7, waiting for this audition. I took *The Complete Works of Shakespeare* out of the library to look for just the right character to play. Perhaps lovely, young, but guy-sick Juliet, *O Romeo, Romeo! Wherefore art thou, Romeo?* Or maybe I could be mean old Lady Macbeth and say things like *thoud'st this* and *wouldst that* and *Fie, My Lord,* and all those other great lines. But then I thought I better lighten up. Yes, yes, I would be the fairy Puck and dance and sing around the stage. Who *to be or not to be*— that was my question.

"I had been sitting in the backyard reading Shakespeare and eating potato chips. I went into the house. I turned on the TV. I fell asleep.

> Who is telling this story? What do you know about her so far?

"*Me thought I heard a voice cry, sleep no more.* No, it was not Macbeth; it was my mother, waking me up. She said it was time to leave for camp. Oh what a morrow that was. I jumped up and grabbed my stuff. It wasn't until we were halfway here that I realized I didn't have my Shakespeare book. I wanted to go home and get it, but my parents said, no, it was too late and we couldn't go back. Truly a Shakespearean tragedy.

"That was yesterday. It takes six hours to drive here. What could I do? I was frazzled.

"It seemed my midsummer's dream had become a nightmare. I had to do something. And you know, Ms. Windsor, I was born to do Shakespeare. I was almost born to *be* Shakespeare. Face facts. My name: Willa S. Speare. That's close enough to Will's name to make us almost related. What's in a name? Let me remind you, Ms. Windsor, what's in a name. *Romeo and Juliet*, Act 2, *That which we call a rose by any other name would smell as sweet.* Maybe I would be just as sweet if I was called Jane or Tiffany, but I wasn't. I'm Willa Susan Speare, born in Stratford, Connecticut, which is not Stratford-on-Avon, Will's hometown, but close enough. Things like these are not just a coincidence.

me:
Willa S. Speare
Stratford, CT

he:
Will Shakespeare
Stratford-on-Avon

"*O woe is me, to have seen what I have seen*— that's *Hamlet*, Act 3—and to flub it.

Who is doing all of the talking on this page?

"Desperation! So I turned to the only person I knew who wouldn't let me down—my bud, Toby. Desperation a second time! He was at baseball camp. Woe is me again. But wait. He has e-mail. Not one second, I exaggerate, maybe two seconds after we got here, I begged to use the camp computer. 'Two minutes,' they said. 'That's it.' And so I e-mailed Toby: To-by or not To-by (as I refer to him). You've got to help me. I left my Shakespeare book at home. My audition is tomorrow. I have two minutes on this computer and that's it! Get thee to a Web site and download me a Shakespeare speech posthaste.

Act 1
Scene 3
backstage

Toby:
(To-by or not To-by)

The computer

The fax machine

"I knew Toby would help. He thinks of life like I do. Well, sorta. I think in terms of acts and scenes—Act 1, Scene 2; or Act 2, Scene 6. He thinks in terms of innings. For me, breakfast could be Act 1. Lunch might be Act 2. Toby, on the other hand, might think of breakfast as the 1st inning and dinner as the 7th inning stretch. His life is so full of sports. Mine is so full of the theater. But we share a passion for excellence. We also live next door to each other.

"Anyway, I finished off my e-mail and bid adieu from Hamlet, *Sweets to the sweets farewell.* That would get Toby. Then I hastened off to the camp's opening ceremonies.

"But I kept sneaking off to the camp office. Nothing! Nothing! Nothing! The evening activities were in full swing. It was fast turning into night and still Toby hadn't gotten back to me. I was frazzled beyond human belief. I gave up. I tried *to sleep, perchance to dream, ah.*

"At 7:00 A.M. I was back at the camp computer. Ah, To-by or not To-by had not disappointed me.

"He wrote: In the words of Yogi Berra, (who has nothing to do with Shakespeare and a lot to do with baseball), 'The game isn't over till it's over.' I faxed thee the info you wanted.

"Sure enough, in the fax machine it lay. Ms. Windsor, I had absolutely no time to even glance at the paper before me. I grabbed it and raced over here to make my audition time.

Why are single quotes used within this paragraph?

Act 1
Scene 4

"But I finally did look . . . when I was up on stage! I realized Toby must have dragged where he should have clicked. Something got transposed as it was not a speech that walked off the pages of Shakespeare. Instead, it was an ad that stumbled off the Internet.

"I read a few lines. *Will's Shakes and Smoothies. Delicious. And So Nutritious.*

"Then I improvised. *O woe is me. O treble woe.* (Suddenly everything Will wrote came back to me like a runaway train.) *Fie, this be'st not Shakespeare's shakes—made from the milk of human kindness. But Will's World Famous Shakes and Smoothies made from the ripest fruit that first falls. Our shake's the thing. To be or not to be. Come have a taste of our quality. Double, double, toil or trouble. Cauldron boil and cauldron bubble. With a hey, ho, our shakes are great! Eye of newt, and toe of frog, wool of bat, and tongue of dog. With a hey, ho, and a merry berry smoothie! Don't wait until tomorrow and tomorrow and tomorrow creeps in this petty pace from day to day. Taste our great shakes and smoothies today! Parting will be such sweet sorrow.*"

"Indeed. Indeed," said Ms. Windsor, getting in what she hoped might be a last word. "You've had quite a comedy of errors. But you remembered one of the greatest lines of all theater: 'the show must go on.' Yes, you improvised, but you had the audience in the palm of your hand. They loved it. They laughed. They applauded. You're terrific. Don't worry, Willa S. Speare, you'll have one of the leads in this summer's show. And as Will would say, *all's well that ends well.*" ○

Stop and Respond

How important is point of view?

Who is telling the story? When a character within a story is telling the story, it is called *first person point of view.* Why do you think it is important for this story to be told in the first person point of view? What do you learn about Willa? Write two or three sentences describing her character from the things she says about herself.

Ad-ventions

Poor Willa ended up with an advertisement for milk shakes instead of a play script. Put your imagination to work and invent an advertisement for a product that could be described by one of the lines from Shakespeare listed below. Draw and name your product and use the quote in your ad.

"Forever and a day . . ." from *As You Like It*
"To sleep, perchance to dream . . ." from *Hamlet*
"Laugh yourself into stitches . . ." from *Twelfth Night*
"In thunder, lightning, or in rain . . ." from *Macbeth*

Notes from King Lear

On a 5" x 8" index card, create a postcard that Willa might send to Toby from Camp King Lear. Put a scene from the camp on one side. On the other, write a message from Willa to Toby, telling about her experiences at camp.

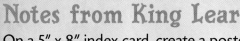

A Walk Through the Classics

by Charles Hirsch

Starting Our Tour:
The Town Bookstore

Follow me, girls and boys, as we step lively into the land where books live. Pick up a classic book and you might find yourself amidst the mythical wonders of ancient Greece and Rome. You might slay fierce dragons that leap out of the pages. Or you may discover how much fun it is to gallop through the classics of the Old West, or to orbit through a space adventure.

Notice that on your right, the classics are standing in alphabetical order by author—from Aesop's *Fables* to Johan David Wyss's *The Swiss Family Robinson*. They're waiting in anticipation on six shelves, each 20 feet long. That's 120 feet of books! On your left is a table stacked with best-selling favorites. There are 20 piles, each about a foot and a half tall. All together that's 150 feet of classic books. (Compare *that* to the Statue of Liberty at 151 feet from toes to torch or to a basketball court at 94 feet long.)

Beyond these classics are aisles filled with both fiction and nonfiction stories and tales. Some of them are just waiting, ready to jump off their shelves and join ranks with the great ones. Did you know that there are more than 90,000 books in print for kids? They're not all classics, of course, but many are classics-in-waiting. Better be sure to wear sneakers. We've got a lot of ground to cover, and this might turn into a full-speed run.

> How does comparing the amount of books to the Statue of Liberty or a basketball court help you imagine how many there are?

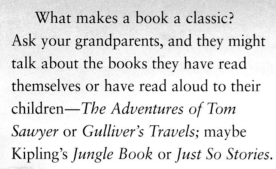

What makes a book a classic? Ask your grandparents, and they might talk about the books they have read themselves or have read aloud to their children—*The Adventures of Tom Sawyer* or *Gulliver's Travels*; maybe Kipling's *Jungle Book* or *Just So Stories.*

Ask your parents, and they might add *The Hobbit.* Or maybe Mom or Dad remember how they identified with Judy Blume's comic *Tales of a Fourth Grade Nothing.* Mom or Dad may call these books classics. Ask a teacher or librarian, and you'll receive even more title suggestions.

Often a quote on the front or back cover gives the reader a clue that the book is a classic— quotes such as, "Deserves a place of honor" *(The Indian in the Cupboard)*; "A rollicking story" *(Pippi Longstocking)*; or "A small stunner" *(Fighting Ground)*. The book may be "A very, very funny story" *(Harriet the Spy)*, or it may not be funny at all, but "A moving and unforgettable story" *(Island of the Blue Dolphins)*. Or maybe the cover comes right out and tells you the book is "The classic fantasy that inspired the famous film" *(The Wizard of Oz)*.

Maybe a classic just has to be old, like *The Life and Adventures of Robinson Crusoe* (1719), *Little Women* (1869), *Treasure Island* (1883), *Anne of Green Gables* (1908), or *The Wind in the Willows* (1908).

But what makes a classic a real page-turner, a first-rate book, a terrific read?

Next Stop:
A Story Well-Told

Plot The plot is the plan of action. It tells what the characters do and what happens to them. It's the thread that holds the story together and makes the reader want to continue reading. Fantasy and adventure hold together the plot of *A Wrinkle in Time,* by Madeleine L'Engle, which leaps from place to place across the universe. The book begins, "It was a dark and stormy night." From that classic first sentence to the end, the plot grows with suspense and mystery.

Setting Classic stories have been set in the past, present, and future. They can take place anywhere and at anytime. The setting may include geography, weather, the news of the day, and the details of everyday life, as it does in *Sarah, Plain and Tall,* a story of pioneers set on the western prairie. Or the story can unfold in a mysterious garden outside a magnificent manor house, as it does in *The Secret Garden.*

Characters Heroes and heroines give us hope that we, too, can do extraordinary things, way beyond our everyday lives of going to school and doing homework. Some characters may be like our best friends. They can make us feel good when we feel really stupid. They say and do things just like we do. Or a character might show us what it was like to be a proper Bostonian girl of the 1850s, as is Lucy in *The Ballad of Lucy Whipple*. Or they may be animals, as are Mole, Ratty, Toad, and Mr. Badger in *The Wind in the Willows*.

Theme The theme is part of the big picture, the larger meaning of the book. The theme of E.B. White's *Charlotte's Web* is the importance of friendship, even though it's the story of how a spider saves the life of a pig. J.K. Rowling tells us that one of the biggest themes of the Harry Potter books is the fight against what she detests most—bigotry and intolerance. (Time will tell, but many say that the Harry Potter books are classics waiting to happen.)

Style Good writing style moves the plot, explores the theme, develops what the characters say and

What are some of the important words on these pages? How do you know?

do, and captures the setting. It's what makes a classic book such a good read. Virginia Hamilton's books have a style graced with imaginative language. She writes, "'Howdy, howdy-howdy,' the children called. The howdys bounced like huge laughter around the hills." The children she is speaking of are the characters we meet in *M.C. Higgins, the Great*, a story about a boy who looks out at his mountainside home from the top of a gleaming 40-foot steel pole.

Natalie Babbitt, often noted for her unique style, loads her books with rich description. Picture Jesse Tuck as she describes him in *Tuck Everlasting:* "He was thin and sunburned, this wonderful boy, with a thick mop of curly brown hair, and he wore his battered trousers and loose, grubby shirt with as much self-assurance as if they were silk and satin."

Our Tour Concludes

Have you decided what makes a classic? A classic could even be a picture book, which unfortunately we haven't had time for on this tour. But think about the generations of kids who have grown up reading *Make Way for Ducklings* or anything by Dr. Seuss—and who continue to read them as teenagers and adults.

Maybe a classic is simply a first-rate book. The famous poet, W. H. Auden, said that after reading a first-rate book, you might say to yourself, "I never knew how I felt. Thanks to this experience, I will never feel the same way again."

What books have YOU read that have changed you? Which author expressed what YOU felt, thought, or wondered, but could never quite say? What books raised YOUR thinking to another level? What books do YOU think are classics in the making? ⭘

Why does the author ask all these questions?

Biggest Winners

The John Newbery Medal is the highest honor given to children's books. Many past Newbery award winners have become classics. Here's a list of some Newbery winners—some will be as popular with your grandchildren as they are today.

Bridge to Terabithia by Katherine Paterson
Dear Mr. Henshaw by Beverly Cleary
Maniac Magee by Jerry Spinelli
Missing May by Cynthia Rylant
Number the Stars by Lois Lowry
Roll of Thunder, Hear My Cry
    by Mildred D. Taylor
Shiloh by Phyllis Reynolds Naylor
Walk Two Moons by Sharon Creech
The Whipping Boy by Sid Fleischman

For a complete list of Newbery award winners, check the Web site www.ala.org/alsc/nquick.html

Stop and Respond

Advertise a Classic-in-Waiting

Choose a favorite book that you think deserves to become a classic. Make a poster to attract other readers to the book. Be sure your poster tells about the important ideas and features of the story. Include illustrations as well.

Touring the Article

Skim the article you just read. List at least three qualities of classic books that the author included. How do these help you decide what is important in a book?

Book Ratings

Rate books you've read recently to decide if they can be considered classics or classics-in-waiting. On a sheet of paper, list three book titles. Use the rating chart below to evaluate each book.

Characteristic	Book 1	Book 2	Book 3
Interesting Plot			
Interesting Setting			
Great Characters			
Worthwhile Theme			
Good Writing Style			

| Rating Scale: | 1 No | 2 A little | 3 Okay | 4 Good | 5 Fantastic! |

The Envelope, Please

Nominate one of your favorite books as a classic. Write a paragraph that explains why the book deserves to be called a classic. Be sure to tell how reading the book changed you or made you better understand something about yourself or your life.

Become a Playwright

Choose a scene from a classic you've enjoyed, and rewrite it in play form. For example, you could retell the scene from *Charlotte's Web* in which Charlotte tries to teach Wilbur how to spin a web. Or you could create a dramatic scene showing how James chases off the Cloud-men in *James and the Giant Peach*.

Fractured Stories

Write and draw a comic strip of a favorite Mother Goose rhyme or fairy tale. First choose a favorite rhyme or tale. Then change or rearrange characters and situations to make a condensed—and slightly wacky—story.

Classical Mix-ups

Have some fun with the classics! Work with two or three friends to identify three books you have all enjoyed. On separate index cards, list the names of several important characters from the books. Do the same for story settings and some important events. Put each set of cards in a separate envelope. Then pick at least one card from each envelope. Write a short story that combines the ideas. For example, you might end up writing about Wilbur the pig "wrinkling" through time to visit Oz.

More Books

Cuffari, Richard. *The Cartoonist*. Viking, 1987.

Greene, Katherine and Richard Greene. *The Man Behind the Magic: The Story of Walt Disney*. Viking, 1998.

Hahn, Don. *Disney's Animation Magic: A Behind-the-Scenes Look at How an Animated Film Is Made*. Hyperion, 1996.

Horn, Pamela (editor). *101 Read-Aloud Classics*. Black Dog & Beventhal, 1995.

Scieszka, Jon. *The True Story of the Three Little Pigs*. Viking, 1989.

Williams, Marcia. *Tales from Shakespeare: Seven Plays*. Candlewick, 1998.

On the Web

About Charles Schultz
http://www.unitedmedia.com/comics/
peanuts/b_artist/index.html

The Bard of Avon
http://www.infoplease.com/spot/
shakespeare1.html

International Museum of Cartoon Art
http://www.cartoon.org/home.htm

Walt Disney and His Works
http://www.intergraffix.com/walt/
options.htm

Across the Curriculum

Research

Investigate the life of a classic author or illustrator, and write a biographical sketch of the person you select. Choose a favorite author or illustrator, an individual mentioned in one of the magazine articles, or someone from the list below.

Louisa May Alcott   Beverly Cleary   Steven Kellogg
Charles Schultz   Chris Van Allsburg   Laura Ingalls Wilder

Art

Create a comic strip of your own. Your strip can be humorous, serious, or full of adventure. List your ideas first, including the dialogue your characters will use and what the main idea of your comic strip will be. You may want to create rough sketches as well. Then put everything together in a final product.

Classic Fun!

Books, stories, and rhymes aren't the only things that can be "classics." Here are some fun things that have been around so long that they are considered classics of their kind.

Tongue Twisters

How much wood would a woodchuck chuck if a woodchuck could chuck wood?

She sells seashells by the seashore.

Peter Piper picked a peck of pickled peppers.

Write a tongue twister of your own. Ask a friend to say it.

Riddles

As round as an apple,
as deep as a cup,
All the king's horses
can't pull it up.
What is it?

Think of a favorite riddle. Ask a friend to solve it.

Knock-Knock Jokes

Knock knock.
    Who's there?
Little old lady.
    Little old lady who?
I didn't know you
could yodel!

Make up a knock-knock joke yourself. Here's a hint: Have "Ken" answer the question. Then make up an answer that starts with "Ken you . . . ?" (Can you . . . ?")

Proverbs don't always agree! Can you match each proverb in the first column with one in the second column that seems to say exactly the opposite?

Proverbs

The early bird catches the worm.

Better late than never.

Too many cooks spoil the broth.

Many hands make light work.

Look before you leap.

He who hesitates is lost.

COMPREHENSION QUARTERLY

CQ⁵

ISSUE C: Determining
Important Ideas and Themes

Scavenger
Hunt

Scavenger Hunt

THINK ABOUT: Determining Important Ideas and Themes

C4

FICTION
Button Hunting
Family members can pass on so much more than just eye color.

C11

NONFICTION
A Fort-unate Find
If you think you've built cool forts before, check this out!

C19

FICTION
The Treasure in Nana's Attic
Kate finds more than she bargained for in a family treasure hunt.

C25

NONFICTION
Sue: A Life Story in Rock
Read about Sue, a Tyrannosaurus rex that currently lives in Chicago.

DETERMINING IMPORTANT IDEAS AND THEMES

The Ring

Good readers know that in order to completely understand a text, they must **determine which ideas are most important.** To do this, they listen to their reader's voice—the one that asks questions or says, "This seems like an important part of the story."

One way readers determine importance is by thinking about what they already know about the subject. The thought bubbles below show how one reader uses his own recollections of a flea market to understand the story and to recognize the most important ideas.

Maria saw her grandmother's straw hat up ahead in the crowd. Maria sighed and caught up to her. A flea market wasn't her idea of fun. The narrow, dusty paths were clogged with bargain hunters. Maria felt trapped beneath the tent that shielded the tables covered with old rag dolls, tattered linens, and rickety furniture.

But then something caught Maria's eye. She peered closely at an ancient ring. At the center of the ring was an oval blue rhinestone.

"That ring was owned by one of the first settlers of these parts." Startled, Maria looked up into the face of an old, tired man. "Whoever wears this is kept safe from danger," he said, smirking.

"Well, it's pretty, even if it doesn't protect me from anything," mumbled Maria. She handed the man fifty cents and then, just as Maria left the table, a teenage boy with an old ladder on his shoulders turned, just missing Maria's head…

> The first few sentences are important—they tell me who the story is about and where the story takes place. The sentence "A flea market wasn't her idea of fun" seems important, too. I felt that way when my mom dragged me to my first flea market.

> Anytime I see the word *but*, I think: watch out, here's a story twist! The sentence about the ring protecting its owner caught my attention. That's a key part of the story, no doubt.

> Is the last sentence a coincidence or not? The ladder missed Maria. That ring seems important to this story.

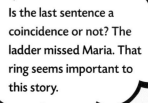

BUTTON HUNTING

by Jacqueline Greene

Will sat on a rickety chair in the cool, damp cellar while Gramps unlatched a rough wooden trunk. Whenever Will visited, his grandfather came up with an adventure they could share, and Will felt certain there was an adventure hidden inside the splintery chest. He leaned in closer.

"We're going on a little treasure hunt," Gramps began, "but it all starts with something I found years ago, inside this very chest." He held the lid open about 2 inches. Will couldn't see anything inside. "Grandma and I stopped at an auction one day," he said. "This trunk was the last item offered, and people were already leaving. The auctioneer rattled on about how the trunk was filled with things nobody had a chance to look at, and he would sell it with everything inside." Gramps chuckled. "Now, that got my attention." He opened the lid a bit wider. "Still, the bidding was slow. When it got to twenty dollars, I offered twenty-three. The auctioneer tried to get higher bids, but no one went even a dollar higher."

"Twenty-three dollars doesn't seem like much," Will said.

"Your grandma thought it was too much," Gramps replied. "She said it was a 'moldy oldie' and didn't want it in the house. That's how it ended up down here." A musty smell came from the open lid. Slowly Gramps pushed open the top and propped it up with an old broom handle.

"Now, some would say there was nothing of value inside," Gramps went on, "but those are folks without any imagination." He reached down into the trunk and pulled out a yellowed envelope and a tiny, carved wooden box.

Grandpa tapped Will's knee with the letter. "What I found here was a treasure worth far more than money."

Carefully, Gramps unfolded the letter and handed it to Will. "Look at the date."

This sounds important! What treasures do you have that are worth more to you than money?

Will held the letter under the bare lightbulb above him. It felt brittle with age. The letter was written in an old-fashioned script, and the ink was brown. At the very top, it said, *August 10, 1862.*

"You know some history," Gramps prompted him. "What was happening in this country in 1862?"

History lessons had all flown out of Will's head, now that it was summer vacation. He concentrated. "The Civil War?" he asked.

Gramps smiled and nodded toward the letter. "Keep reading."

"*Dear Sister,*" Will read aloud. "*We have traveled as far as the vast state of Pennsylvania, and luckily have seen no military action. The people here are kindly. Yesterday, a farmer killed two hogs and we feasted on fresh meat. It was a rare treat after so many days of eating dried rations from my knapsack. Some days, I live only on bitter coffee and bread.*

"*A trio of young women from the village came to our camp, asking the men for a button from their uniform. Seeing I was an officer, one young lady fancied my gilt buttons with the insignia of New York State. She boldly offered a kiss in exchange for a souvenir.*

"*I decided that if the buttons of this ragged uniform are in any way desirable, then you should have one for safekeeping. I declined the kiss, telling the young miss that I would rather trade all my buttons for one kind look from my*

dear sister at home. She was much offended and left to find a kinder soldier than I. So I sat in my tent to write you these words and enclose a button from my sleeve. Keep it for me until I return, and I shall feel well protected.

Your brother,

Henry (Lt. Henry Waters, U.S. Army)"

"I can't believe I'm holding a letter written by a Union soldier," Will said. He was afraid to refold it because it seemed so fragile. Gramps emptied the box into his hand. Carved leaves twined across the top and along the sides. The inside was lined with velvet. When Gramps opened his palm, Will saw a gold button with the state seal of New York. "Is this the button he sent?" Will's eyes widened. He held the button to the light. Its gold finish was a bit worn, but it still shined.

Why might Lt. Waters' letter and button be so important to preserve?

"That letter and button were the beginning of a treasure hunt for me," Gramps said. He took another box from the trunk and opened it. Loose buttons rolled around inside. Brass and gilt, each had a different design. "I've been looking for Civil War buttons ever since," he said. "I find them at flea markets and auctions, and even sometimes at yard sales."

"How did people get them?" Will asked. "These buttons are almost 150 years old!"

"Some were found on battlefields," Gramps explained. "And some were saved by the soldiers themselves. Sometimes soldiers traded buttons from their uniforms to seal a friendship. As the war dragged on, surviving soldiers stole them from the dead because they didn't have enough buttons left to close their own jackets. At the end of the war, Confederate soldiers surrendered at Union camps. An officer would formally pardon them and send them home. But first, every Confederate soldier was stripped of his buttons."

"Didn't the Confederate soldiers want to keep them?" Will asked.

Confederate Infantry

Union Artillery

Union Cavalry

Union Ordnance

"It was humiliating for some, and many were filled with anger. But they were tough men, and they stood still while a Union soldier sliced off the buttons with a pocketknife. They had to allow it or go to prison, instead of heading home. At the end of that war, every soldier wanted nothing more than to get home."

Will's grandfather closed the trunk and switched off the light. They headed back upstairs, and Gramps set the letter and button box on the kitchen table. He poured each of them a glass of icy lemonade. Then he handed Will a thick book. It was titled *The Collector's Guide to Civil War Items*. Will opened it to the section on buttons. There were so many kinds! Each was pictured, and an explanation described both Union and Confederate buttons worn by soldiers and officers.

"Tomorrow we're heading off to a giant flea market," Gramps said. "They claim it's the biggest one in the country! And we're going to hunt for buttons."

That night, Will could hardly sleep. He held a flashlight under the covers and read everything the book said about Civil War buttons. Sharpshooters wore rubber buttons so the sun wouldn't reflect off them and give away their hiding places. Most Union soldiers wore brass buttons with the picture of an eagle with outstretched wings and a shield on its chest. A letter on the shield showed which division the soldier was in. *I* was for "Infantry." An *A* designated "Artillery." The letter *C* was for Cavalry soldiers on horseback. Officers had different buttons made of gilt, like the one Lt. Waters had sent to his sister. Will saw that ordnance officers, who directed the cannons, had buttons with crossed cannons and bombshells on them.

> What important information has Will learned about Civil War buttons?

At the flea market, a small field was lined with rows of booths. Will and Gramps went from one to another and sifted through boxes of small items. Will found lots of old buttons, but none from the Civil War. As they browsed, Will became separated from Gramps. Maybe he could find a button by himself and surprise his grandfather. The sign over one area said "Largest Dealer of Civil War Items." Will searched through every box and container there. He checked display cases. There wasn't a single button.

But at the bottom of a box filled with belt buckles, Will spotted something he thought Gramps would like instead of a button. It might be just as interesting.

"How much for this?" he asked the dealer. The man hardly seemed to know what it was, but Will had seen it in the collector's book last night. His heart was beating, hoping it wouldn't cost too much.

The dealer held the flat, tarnished brass item in his hand. A half-inch slit was cut

Think back to a treasure you found. How did you feel? How might Will be feeling now?

through the middle with a round hole at the center for the button. "A dollar will be enough," he said.

Will couldn't believe his luck. He paid the man and found Gramps sitting on a bench.

Sweat beaded on Gramps forehead. "I think the 'Biggest Flea Market in America,' really isn't," Gramps said. "Let's go home."

"I'm ready," Will smiled. "But I did get you one thing." He handed his discovery to Gramps.

"A button board!" he exclaimed.

Will turned it over. On the bottom, faintly stamped, was "Lieutenant Dan Ingram, 1st Infantry."

"I learned about this in your book! It's to slide over a button, so the soldier can polish it without getting his uniform dirty."

Grandpa patted Will on the back. "Now you've got a button treasure of your own," he said. "I've been looking for someone to share this with. I'm warning you, though. Once you start, it's a tough habit to break!" He grinned at Will. "Happy hunting!" ◯

A Top-Ten List

Survey your classmates and find out what they collect. Create a top-ten list of collectibles for your classroom.

Your Thoughts

Will's grandfather said his trunk contained "a treasure worth far more than money." With a partner, debate your reaction to this statement. Refer back to the story and give at least three solid arguments to support your position.

Catalog It

Think of an object in your house, such as an old poster, a political button, a piece of furniture, or a childhood memento. Create a catalog entry that persuades the owner of a flea market that the object has value. Your catalog entry should include the following information: the date the object was made, its relationship to a period or event in history (or to its owner), and a physical description. You might also want to include a sketch of the object.

Vulture

Perhaps the most famous scavengers of all, vultures eat the carcasses of dead animals left by other scavengers, birds, or mammals. Although vultures have powerful bills, they cannot easily tear the hides of large animals. And their talons are too weak to use in attacks against live animals. So they often wait until other scavengers have had their fill.

Spider Beetle

To the spider beetle, a meal can be grain, dried fruits, meats, feathers, and even books. Spider beetles are scavengers that "bug" people who run warehouses, grain mills, museums, and homes. Athough they are considered insects, they are called spider beetles because some types look like the eight-legged critters.

Animal Recyclers?

People scavenge for buried treasures, for objects to create art, or to add to their collections. In the animal world, scavengers help keep nature in balance. Before you say "yuck," consider this: scavengers clean the environment by eating the dead bodies of animals left by predators.

Painted Turtles

Ponds stay healthy, in part, because of painted turtles. They feed on vegetation and dead animal matter that would otherwise clog ponds. Painted turtles spend most of their time in the water, but often sun themselves on rocks or logs. After all, keeping a pond clean is hard work!

Burying Beetle

When a burying beetle finds a dead animal, it buries it by digging underneath the body. The body slowly sinks deeper until it is completely buried. The female beetle lays her eggs in a tunnel near the body. When the eggs hatch, the larvae eat the rest of the dead animal.

A FORT-UNATE FIND!

by Renee Skelton

Randy Jones loves stuff that other people don't want. He has a barn full of aged wood, old doors, broken chairs, used license plates, creaky shutters, and antique signs. Jones has been a collector since childhood. As a young boy, he filled up his family's garage with all sorts of junk. His mom finally put her foot down and said "enough." But as an adult, Jones can scavenge all he wants. Now he uses what he finds to build children's playhouses.

> What kinds of things do you scavenge for?

Mr. Jones has built more than 100 playhouses in the past ten years. No two are alike. Instead, each matches the interests of the child who plays in it. The playhouse might be a fort, a schoolhouse, a general store, a hot dog stand—or anything else that strikes a kid's fancy. No matter what they are, all of Jones's playhouses are alike in one way. They're all made from stuff he has scavenged—stuff that other people have thrown away.

One Person's JUNK Is Another Person's Treasure

Jones began building playhouses almost by accident ten years ago. "I had a whole barn full of junk and I didn't know what to do with it," he remembers. "So I figured, well, I'm going to build playhouses for my children." He built one for his son Bradley, now 17. He built another for his daughter Katelyn, now 15. A friend saw the playhouses. He asked Jones to build one for his kids, too. Jones did, and a new business took to the sky. Now when kids see

Read on to find out how important his children's playhouses became.

him around town, they say, "Hey, there's the fort fairy!"

Before he started to build playhouses, Randy Jones had another career. He was a swimsuit designer for many years. He has retired from that career and now combines his love of kids, art, and scavenging in his new career. "I've had more fun doing this than anything else I've ever done," says Jones. "Just to see the smiles on the kids' faces, it's fantastic."

A small wooden fort stands in the corner of P.J. Kadzik's yard in Arlington, Virginia. Jones built it three years ago. The fort has a lookout tower. It also has a trapdoor for quick get-aways. Visitors walk over a narrow drawbridge to reach the fort. "It wasn't much fun in the backyard, just running around," says 11-year-old P.J. "So

I asked my mom if I could have a fort or something." P.J. got the fort he wanted for his birthday. Now he's on top of the world when he plays in it. "Sometimes we play tag, and sometimes we play hide-and-seek," P.J. says. "My favorite part is the trapdoor and the ladder because you can go out and sneak attack and things like that."

How does Mr. Jones find the junk he turns into playhouses? He is always on the lookout for old things near his home in Arlington. Many farms in nearby Maryland and Virginia have been sold to build new houses. When that happens, people tear down old barns and other farm buildings. So Jones takes wood and other junk that would be thrown away. He gets old banisters, doors, and light fixtures from old city houses that are torn down, too.

Jones also searches the streets on days when people put out old furniture and other trash for pick up. He makes the rounds just ahead of the garbage trucks. He picks out the stuff he can use and throws it into his truck. Someday these trash treasures will become parts of new playhouses.

Randy Jones is a scavenger wherever he goes. If he's driving down the street, he's on the lookout as well. Bouncing along the streets of

Use what you have read so far to support your thoughts about Randy Jones and his scavenging.

Arlington in his truck, Jones spots a small wooden file cabinet on the curb. It's garbage to most people, but not to Jones. "I would take that and paint it the favorite color of a kid. I would put his name on it and birth date and put it inside a playhouse," he says as he inspects the curbside treasure.

Putting It All TOGETHER

Mr. Jones sits down and talks to each child before building a playhouse. Shooting the breeze gives him a good idea of what his customer is like. They fill out a questionnaire, too. That gives Jones additional information. What is the child's favorite color or lucky number? Does the child have a favorite sport or hobby? Jones then uses the information to design the perfect playhouse for that boy or girl.

Jones has learned a thing or two about what kids like over the years. So there are three features most playhouses include. "First, there should be a ramp that goes to it," Jones explains. "Second, they get a trapdoor or a secret door. Third, there has to be a spy tower.

Every kid wants a spy tower. And toilet seat windows are big, especially for boys."

Jones writes almost nothing down when he plans the playhouses. "It's all up here," he says, pointing to his head. Once he has a rough idea, he takes four to five months to gather materials. He collects stuff for several playhouses at a time. The "junk" is stored in a Delaware barn where he makes the playhouses. "I have stalls in the barn," says Jones. "I'll put each child's name on one of the stalls. And every time I see something that would be good for that particular playhouse, I'll stick it in there." If he's making a playhouse for a child who likes boats and swimming, he'll look for nautical things. He might see an old porthole or a boat paddle. He'll throw that into the stall in his barn for that playhouse. By the time he's ready to build the playhouse, he has all kinds of junk that's just right.

What important information does Mr. Jones use in creating his playhouses?

When it's time to start building, Jones uses his imagination to make something wonderful out of the old junk. Aged barn wood becomes playhouse walls. Old banisters and wood become wrap-around porches and balconies. Toilet seats and picture frames become windows. Pieces of old beds turn into chairs and tables. Old license plates, doorknockers, old instruments, and antique signs decorate walls.

Jones does most of the work himself at the barn, but a couple of helpers lend a hand. Mr. Jones travels to the playhouse location one month ahead of time to build a platform for it. Then he returns to Delaware and builds the playhouse itself. That takes a few days. He builds it in about 23 pieces. When a playhouse is done, he loads the parts into his delivery truck. Jones drives to his customer's home and unloads the parts of the playhouse in the yard. Then it takes him two days to put it all together.

Randy Jones's playhouses aren't cheap. They cost at least $3,000—more depending on how elaborate they become. The Vandenberg family didn't mind the expense, however. They own an original Jones's playhouse. "I wanted to do something special for Melissa," says her dad, Larry Vandenberg. "I tried to come up with some sort of design, but just couldn't come up with anything." Then he saw one of Jones's playhouses and called him. "I told him what I was trying to do. He said, 'Oh, I see what you want,' and he sketched it out. He came up with all the signs and decorations and stuff."

For 9-year-old Melissa Vandenberg, Jones used a general store theme. A weathered sign, "Sasha's General Store" (Sasha is her nickname), hangs above the porch. Inside there's a balcony. There are also a couple of secret doors and ladders. Because Melissa likes gymnastics, bars and rings hang outside. The walls have colorful old metal signs and posters. The playhouse also has a toilet seat window, an antique doorknocker, and a spy tower.

The Perfect JOB

To him, Jones's job is perfect. He builds his playhouses during the week so he can spend weekends at home with his wife (a fifth-grade teacher) and his two children. This kind of schedule also gives him time to work on his own home. Randy Jones has built his own house with—what else?—antiques he has scavenged over the years!

If you would like to see more of the playhouses Mr. Jones has built, visit his Web site at www.katelynskastles.com.

Stop and Respond

Your Own Fort

If you could design your own private fort, what would it look like? Make a list of different objects you might find at a garage sale or flea market to use in the design of your fort. How could you use them, as Randy Jones did, to design your own fort? Draw a diagram of your fort, using labels to point out interesting features.

 **to the Fort Fairy**

Some people might say that the "Fort Fairy," Randy Jones, is a lot like the fairy godmother in the Cinderella story because he uses everyday objects to make children's dreams come true. Write a short poem that describes the real-life magic that Mr. Jones creates with his forts.

Remember WHEN

Tell a friend or write in your journal about a special fort you once built or a favorite place you played in when you were younger. Describe five things that made it special, including what it was made of; where it was; and the smells, sounds, or even tastes that you associate with it.

HUNTING FOR WORDS

Artists often use their imaginations to discover works of art or treasures in everyday objects, just like Randy Jones does when he scavenges for fort materials.

Word lovers use their imaginations, too, as they hunt for new words. One word game you can play to hunt for words is called Anagrams. To play, you make a word by scrambling the letters of another word. Some words can be rearranged into two or more words. For example, the word *staple* can be changed into *pastel, petals, pleats,* or *plates.* Try your hand at these, finding at least one new word for each:

ache	earn	stayed
bale	lime	untied
door	please	wolves

Can you come up with your own words for an Anagram game? Challenge a friend with your game.

Another fun word game is to try to figure out a mystery compound word based on two clues. The first clue describes the first part of the compound word, and the second clue describes the second part of the compound word. For example, the clues for the word *understand* would look like this:

Part 1 of the word = not over, but _____ . Part 2 = not to sit, but to _____ .

Scan the articles in this issue for five compound words. Create clues like the one above for each part of the word. See if you can stump a friend with clues for the compound words you found. How long did it take your friend to figure out the compound words?

DETERMINING IMPORTANT IDEAS AND THEMES

The Ancient Treasures of Pompeii

When we tell someone about a movie we just saw, we focus on what we think was the most important part—like the interesting characters or the cool special effects. The same is true when we read—we consider each bit of new information to **determine the most important ideas**. For example, we might decide that one character's solution to a problem is the key part of a story. Or we might pay special attention when we read words like *first, next,* and *last.*

Recently I had to write a report about what I want to be when I grow up. I want to be an archaeologist! My dream is to excavate treasures at Pompeii.

I read an encyclopedia article about Pompeii and included only the most important information as part of my report. I jotted the most important facts on note cards and ranked them in order of importance. The article helped me to explain why I want to be an archaeologist. The most important fact that I used from the encyclopedia was that only three-fourths of the city has been uncovered! Maybe one day I'll be on a team to uncover the rest. Can you find two other facts that I might have included in my report?

Think about determining importance when you read other things today. How did you decide what was most important in today's science lesson? Or in the directions to your math assignment?

Pompeii

(*pahm PAY*) was an ancient city in Italy that was destroyed after the eruption of Mt. Vesuvius in 79 A.D. For 1,500 years, the city lay buried beneath heaps of ashes and cinders. In 1748, German archaeologist Johan Joachim Winckelmann discovered the city. Experts believe that the ashes and cinders helped preserve the site. Since Winckelmann's discovery, several excavations have told scientists much about the city and about ancient Rome.

About three-quarters of Pompeii has been uncovered. Visitors can see buildings as they stood almost 2,000 years ago, and many Pompeiian objects are displayed in the National Museum in Naples.

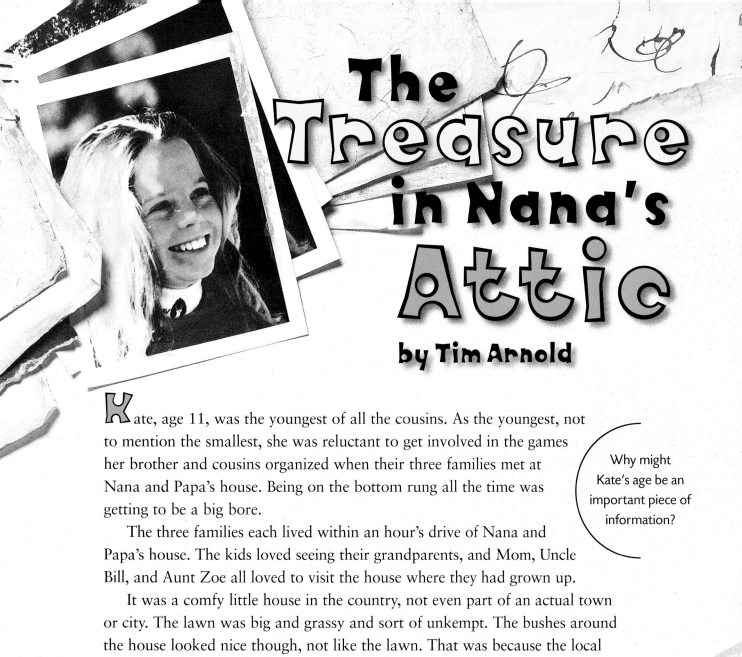

The Treasure in Nana's Attic

by Tim Arnold

Kate, age 11, was the youngest of all the cousins. As the youngest, not to mention the smallest, she was reluctant to get involved in the games her brother and cousins organized when their three families met at Nana and Papa's house. Being on the bottom rung all the time was getting to be a big bore.

The three families each lived within an hour's drive of Nana and Papa's house. The kids loved seeing their grandparents, and Mom, Uncle Bill, and Aunt Zoe all loved to visit the house where they had grown up.

It was a comfy little house in the country, not even part of an actual town or city. The lawn was big and grassy and sort of unkempt. The bushes around the house looked nice though, not like the lawn. That was because the local deer were always nibbling on them, whether the bushes needed a trim or not.

Today, however, was only a day visit, as it usually was when all three families came at once. And today's activity was a scavenger hunt. The two oldest had come up with the idea. The adults had agreed to make a list of interesting things for the children to find in and around the house and to write clues as to their whereabouts. Copies were made and distributed to everyone. Instead of breaking up into teams as you usually should in a scavenger hunt, everyone was on their own.

> Why might Kate's age be an important piece of information?

As usual, Kate fell behind early. She found the first item without too much difficulty. The clue read: "With a thumping roar, I announce your presence at the door." It was pretty clear to Kate that it was the brass doorknocker shaped like a lion's head. Then, despite trying desperately to find at least one of the next four or five items, she found herself stuck, unable to make sense of *any* of the clues.

Kate was wandering around the upstairs of Nana and Papa's house with the crumpled list in her hand, when she came upon the door to the attic. Everyone else had to stoop way down to get in, but not Kate. This advantage, as far as Kate could see, was one of the few that came with being small. That, along with the fact that the attic was far removed from the noise of the others finding the items on their lists, was why Kate went up the attic steps and began to nose around.

Her eyes settled almost immediately on a small, dark, wooden chest nestled among some cardboard boxes in the light of the attic's single window. This chest looked thoroughly different from (and far more interesting than) the rest of the junk that cluttered the attic. It didn't have much dust on it, as if someone had opened it fairly recently. So Kate opened it, too.

Its contents were not spectacular, at least not at first glance. Kate was half expecting something of obvious monetary value, like jewelry, or coins, or a family heirloom—something at least a *little* treasure-ish—but no. Instead there were bundles of letters held together with rubber bands and a lot of photographs of people she didn't recognize. The top one was of an interesting-looking young woman with her arms around the waist of a young man. The couple was standing in the sand with the ocean behind them. She turned the picture over, and written in blue ink on the back was "Helen and Dave—Moon Beach, 1941."

What might be the importance of these letters and photographs?

Helen, she knew, was Nana's real first name, the one everyone but *her* children and grandchildren called her. Kate had seen pictures of Nana when she was a young girl. But this Dave . . . who was *he*? And why should Nana/Helen have her arms around his waist like that? And what business did she have looking so . . . so . . . so *smitten* by someone who wasn't Papa (whose name was Edgar, not Dave)? Kate felt a wave of genuine annoyance, anger, and even betrayal surge inside her. How could Nana have done this? Kate decided she would get to the bottom of it. She closed the lid of the little wooden chest and went down the attic stairs to find the others, taking the chest with her.

Everyone was gathered in the living room. Santos was about to be crowned King of the Scavenger Hunt. He had found all the items on the list first, just ahead of his very competitive brother, Evan. Kate marched into the middle of the room, firmly clutching the chest. She turned to where Nana was sitting. "Nana," she asked accusingly, "who is this Dave person with you in this picture?"

Nana did not reply right away. She looked angered by Kate's question, then her face softened.

"First, Kate," Nana said gently, but firmly, "those are *my* letters and photos and you really shouldn't have been looking through them without my permission."

How is Nana's reaction to Kate's question important or unimportant?

Kate reddened. "I'm sorry, Nana," she whispered.

"Come sit here with me, Kate," said Nana. Kate was apprehensive, but was glad for the chance to cozy up with Nana in the big armchair.

"Dave was my fiancé," she said.

"You were engaged to him? To marry?" asked Kate.

"Yes," said Nana.

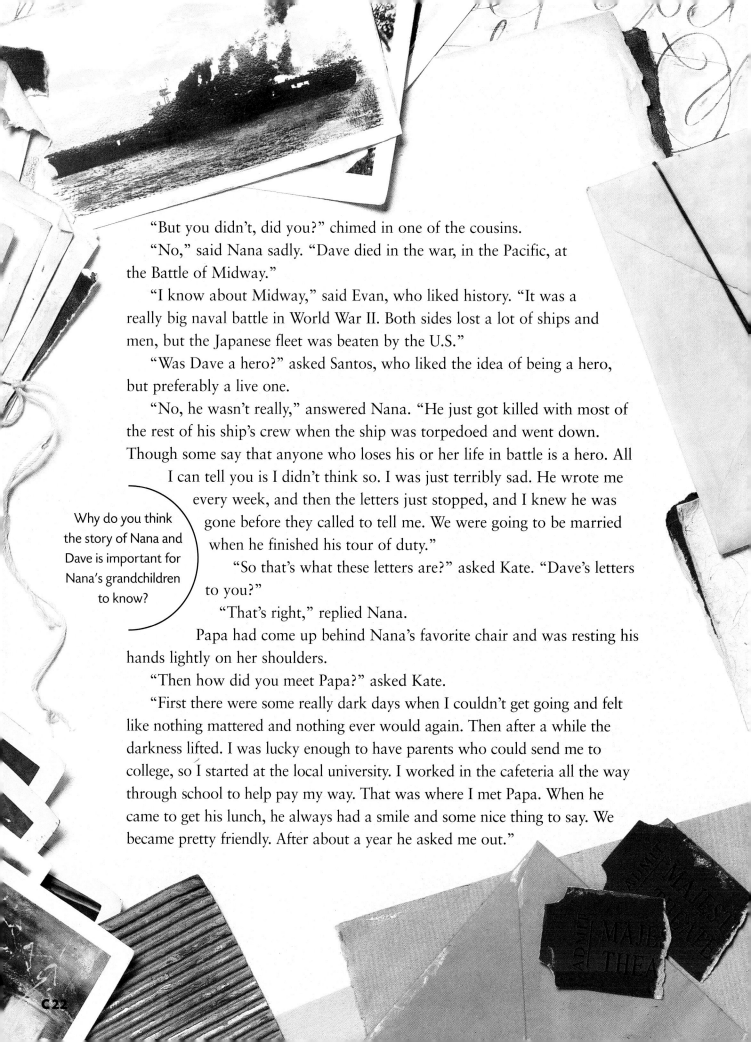

"But you didn't, did you?" chimed in one of the cousins.

"No," said Nana sadly. "Dave died in the war, in the Pacific, at the Battle of Midway."

"I know about Midway," said Evan, who liked history. "It was a really big naval battle in World War II. Both sides lost a lot of ships and men, but the Japanese fleet was beaten by the U.S."

"Was Dave a hero?" asked Santos, who liked the idea of being a hero, but preferably a live one.

"No, he wasn't really," answered Nana. "He just got killed with most of the rest of his ship's crew when the ship was torpedoed and went down. Though some say that anyone who loses his or her life in battle is a hero. All I can tell you is I didn't think so. I was just terribly sad. He wrote me every week, and then the letters just stopped, and I knew he was gone before they called to tell me. We were going to be married when he finished his tour of duty."

Why do you think the story of Nana and Dave is important for Nana's grandchildren to know?

"So that's what these letters are?" asked Kate. "Dave's letters to you?"

"That's right," replied Nana.

Papa had come up behind Nana's favorite chair and was resting his hands lightly on her shoulders.

"Then how did you meet Papa?" asked Kate.

"First there were some really dark days when I couldn't get going and felt like nothing mattered and nothing ever would again. Then after a while the darkness lifted. I was lucky enough to have parents who could send me to college, so I started at the local university. I worked in the cafeteria all the way through school to help pay my way. That was where I met Papa. When he came to get his lunch, he always had a smile and some nice thing to say. We became pretty friendly. After about a year he asked me out."

"A year!" exclaimed Santos. "Papa, were you crazy? You waited a whole year to ask her out?"

Papa laughed good-naturedly. "It might have been longer," he said. "I noticed her before she noticed me. Anyway, I heard through a friend that she'd lost her fiancé in the war, so I didn't want to press. And it always took me a while to work up the nerve to ask a girl out, especially one as beautiful as your nana was."

Nana rolled her eyes, but smiled. "We dated all through college, and when Edgar graduated and got his first job with Fleet Oil, he proposed."

"And you accepted?" asked Kate.

"Of course," said Nana. "I loved him a lot, and his prospects seemed pretty solid."

"What about *your* prospects?" asked Kate, with a note of defiance in her voice.

"Well," said Nana. "Some women *were* starting careers back then, but I just wasn't one of them. I did what *I* wanted to."

"And as a result, *we're* all here," Santos reminded the rest of the cousins. "Otherwise, we'd all be different people sitting in a different house somewhere."

Everyone laughed.

"Let us now continue the coronation," announced Nana, "of Santos, the King of the Scavenger Hunt."

"And I propose," said Papa, "that we also crown Kate *Princess* of the Scavenger Hunt, for having brought Nana's stories to us."

And so the coronation took place, and Kate, despite her undisputed smallness, couldn't have felt any better . . . or bigger. ○

What information did you feel was most important in this story? Why?

Stop and Respond

Get a Clue

Imagine that your whole class is planning a scavenger hunt like the one described in the story. With three or four other students, find five interesting (but not that hard to find!) objects around your classroom or school to include in the hunt. Work together to create clever clues like the one for the lion doorknocker. Share your clues with the rest of the class.

Change the Ending

How might the story have ended if Kate had found something else in the chest, such as an old record, a military uniform, or a surprising news clipping? Think of another interesting object that Kate might have found in the dusty old chest. In your journal, tell how the story might have ended if she had found this instead of the picture.

You Decide

At first, Kate's grandmother seemed angry that Kate had opened the hidden-away chest. But by the end of the story, Kate's discovery had given the family an opportunity to share some of its history. Even so, do you think Kate was right to open the chest without permission? Write two or three paragraphs explaining your opinion.

SUE
A LIFE STORY IN ROCK

by Lisa Klobuchar

Who would have ever expected that a dead horse and a flat tire would lead to the discovery of the most famous dinosaur in the world today? Odd as it sounds, in 1990, these were the two key coincidences that led fossil hunter Susan Hendrickson to the pile of bones that is now known the world over as "Sue," the 42-foot-long *Tyrannosaurus rex* that "lives" at the Field Museum of Natural History in Chicago.

Being a *T.rex,* Sue is special enough—only about 20 partial *T.rex* skeletons have ever been found. She might even be called the queen of this special group. With her 250 bones, Sue is 90 percent complete—the most complete *T.rex* ever found. What's more, some of Sue's bones have never been seen before. Sue has provided scientists with more clues to the life of the *T.rex* than any other fossil found to date.

Susan Hendrickson, Sue's discoverer, was part of a team of fossil hunters at the Black Hills Institute of Geological Research. The Institute had operated a dinosaur dig site on the Ruth Mason ranch near Faith, South Dakota, since the late 1970s. During that time, the fossil hunters had discovered hundreds of partial skeletons of plant-eating hadrosaurs, or duckbill dinosaurs. But finding a *T.rex* skeleton was a prize that the Black Hills fossil hunters only dreamed of. Susan Hendrickson once told a reporter that they'd often joke that they would find a saber-tooth cat skeleton. "But a *T.rex?*" she said. "You don't even joke about that. It's too far-fetched."

The 1990 digging season at the Ruth Mason site began in midsummer. On one of their first days there, the team found a dead horse on their way to the dig site. After asking around for several days, they finally tracked down the horse's owner, a neighboring rancher named Maurice Williams. When Williams came to collect the horse's body, the fossil hunters showed him around the dig site. Williams, fascinated by their work, told them that his ranch had a lot of cliffs and stone outcroppings (the part of a rock formation that appears at the surface of the ground). He invited them to come and have a look around.

What clues does the author give you about the importance of Williams' ranch?

THE DISCOVERY

Although the Black Hills team spent long hours under the blazing South Dakota sun digging earth, moving heavy rocks, and breathing in dust, they found time to visit the Williams' ranch a few times. On one of these visits, Susan Hendrickson spotted a sandstone cliff in the distance. Something about that cliff spoke to her. At the end of a day of heavy digging, however, she was always too tired to make the hike across Williams' land.

Here's where the lucky flat tire comes in. Two days before the dig was to end for the year, the Institute's truck got a flat. Some team members decided to drive into town to get it fixed. They invited Susan to come along, but she decided instead to check out the Williams' property.

The morning of August 14, 1990, was unusual for a South Dakota summer day—the landscape was blanketed in fog. Susan set out with her dog for the 7-mile hike to the cliff, but she lost her bearings in the fog. After two hours of hiking, she was back to where she started.

But Susan Hendrickson didn't give up. She sat down and waited for the fog to clear. When it did, she made a beeline for the cliffs. Once there, she began walking slowly along with her eyes glued to the ground. She didn't have to search for long—a small pile of bone pieces lay at the base of the cliff. Wondering where they'd come from, Susan looked up and spied something even more interesting. Three vertebrae (spine bones) and part of a

Why do you think Susan Hendrickson was so determined to check out Williams' ranch?

femur (thigh bone) had been exposed on the cliff face.

Susan knew enough about dinosaur bones to know that these vertebrae had the distinctive shape found only in meat-eaters. These bones seemed to be from a creature that was very big. Susan knew that *T.rex*, a major meat-eating dinosaur, had lived in this region 65 million years ago. Were these bones in the cliff face from a *T.rex*?

Why might the information in this paragraph be important to remember? Read on to find out.

Susan took the fossil samples back to camp. There, her associates confirmed her suspicion. The bones *did* belong to a *T.rex*. The way that the bones were positioned in the cliff face made it clear that they were articulated, meaning they were preserved in the same position that they had occupied in the live animal. This meant that Susan may have found a complete skeleton. If so, it would be the discovery of a lifetime.

The celebration would have to wait, however. There was a lot of hard work to be done. The fossils, buried under almost 30 feet of hard rock and earth, had to be removed by hand with picks and shovels. For four solid days, the fossil hunters labored in the 110-degree heat just to reach the bone layer. Then they had to prepare the fossils for removal. This job involved carefully chipping away as much of the matrix, or surrounding rock, as possible and covering the exposed fossils with a jacket of plaster for protection.

By September 1, the last of the *T.rex* fossils were ready to move. The last block was loaded, weighing about five tons. It contained the skull, pelvis, right leg, some foot bones and ribs, vertebrae, and other bones. Then Sue was driven to the Black Hills Geological Institute's headquarters in Hill City, South Dakota.

For the next two years, the Black Hills staff worked on the painstaking job of freeing Sue's bones from the matrix. Their excitement and hopes grew; a find like Sue would bring fame and fortune to the Institute. They might be able to answer questions that scientists had been asking for years. They also believed their dream of

What Sue Has Taught Us So Far

- *T.rex* was slower than first thought. It was once believed that *T.rex* could cruise at 40 miles per hour or more. But Sue's foot bones show that she moved like an elephant. Her top speed was only about 15 miles per hour.
- Meat-eating dinosaurs were closely related to birds. Sue has several features shared by birds: a huge wishbone, birdlike nerve pathways, and birdlike leg muscles. This is further evidence that today's birds may have evolved from dinosaurs.

What Sue Has Not Revealed

- Despite the birdlike features, Sue's remains give no clues to whether she was scaly like a reptile or feathery like a bird.
- Although Sue is commonly called a "she," scientists have concluded that Sue's bones do not prove that she is really a female.
- Scientists have argued for years about whether dinosaurs were warm-blooded like birds and mammals or cold-blooded like fish and reptiles. For now, this question still remains a mystery.

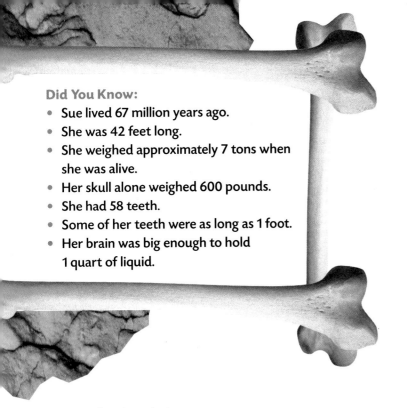

Did You Know:

- Sue lived 67 million years ago.
- She was 42 feet long.
- She weighed approximately 7 tons when she was alive.
- Her skull alone weighed 600 pounds.
- She had 58 teeth.
- Some of her teeth were as long as 1 foot.
- Her brain was big enough to hold 1 quart of liquid.

having their own museum was sure to become a reality. As word spread of the remarkable find, scientists, reporters, and interested citizens flocked to the Institute—more than 2,000 visitors came over the next year and a half.

A LEGAL BATTLE

On the morning of May 14, 1992, the staff at the Institute was greeted with some unexpected visitors—the FBI. The U.S. government had decided that Sue should be in its possession because the bones were found on land that partially belonged to the government. The staff could only watch in despair as government agents and soldiers packed up Sue's bones and carted them away.

How might the FBI's visit prove to be important information in Sue's story?

Years of legal battles followed. In the end, the courts determined that the fossils did indeed belong to the U.S. government, which held them on behalf of Maurice Williams. Sue went up for auction on October 4, 1997. The Black Hills Institute wanted very much to buy Sue back, but they only had $1.2 million to spend—not nearly enough. In the end, the Field Museum of Natural History in Chicago, Illinois, bought the fossils for $8.36 million.

And so, the staff at the Field Museum finished preparing Sue's bones for display. Over two and a half years later, on May 17, 2000, she was unveiled to the public. Today, and for years to come, Sue will be available for the public to admire and for scientists to study. Who knows what other secrets she will reveal?

ASK QUESTIONS

This article has lots of information about Sue, the famous *T.rex*. But you probably have more questions about Sue, her name, and why the fossils were taken away from the Black Hills Institute of Geological Research. In your journal, list five questions you would like to ask Ms. Hendrickson.

CREATE A MUSEUM POSTER

Sue is one cool dinosaur. But why is she so important to science? Gather information from the article and from news or magazine articles you find in the library. Then create a poster describing why Sue is the "queen" of the *T.rex* fossils.

TO WHOM SHOULD SUE BELONG?

What was your reaction when you learned that the United States government took Sue's remains from the Black Hills Institute? To whom should the fossils belong? In a group, discuss your opinions.

Cool Collections

Talk to a friend about his or her interesting collection. It might be a collection of coins, stamps, insects, toys, buttons, or postcards. Start by jotting down a list of questions that will help you find out why the person started the collection, where he or she found the items, and what the person feels is unique about the collection. Record the answers and use them to write a short article for your school newspaper.

Treasure-Hunt Time Line

As you read in the story about Sue, the *T. rex,* it can take a long time from the first discovery of a fossil to the time it is brought out to be seen by the public. The same is true of sunken ships and pharaohs' tombs. Create a time line that details the major steps that must take place to bring an important discovery to the public eye. If you want, you can illustrate your time line. Then share it with the class.

Recycling Rap

You know about the benefits of recycling, reusing plastic containers, and refusing to use products that hurt the environment. Why not share what you know in the form of a song? Use rhyme and rhythm to encourage people to be ecoscavengers—to use existing products (like plastic containers, leftover food, and scraps of paper) in works of art, in gardens, and in the home.

More Books

Laubenstein, Karen. *Archaeology Smart Jr.: Discovering History's Buried Treasures.* Princeton Review, 1997.

Lourie, Peter. *Lost Treasure of the Inca.* Boyds Mills Press, 1999.

Oswald, Diane L. *101 Great Collectibles for Kids.* Krause Publications, 1997.

On the Web

An Internet Treasure Hunt
http://www.cybersurfari.com

Dinosaur Dig Locations and Information
http://www.pbs.org/wgbh/nova/trex

American Treasures
http://www.lcweb.loc.gov/exhibits/
    treasures

Across the Curriculum

Art

A fun way to learn about art is to go on an art museum scavenger hunt. You don't even need to go to a real museum! Make a copy of the list below. Look at art books and magazines or museum sites on the Internet to find a painting, sculpture, or other piece of art that has one of the features on the list. As you check off each list item, note the title of the artwork, the name of the artist, and when it was created. The first person in the class to complete his or her list "wins." Remember this game if you ever get the chance to visit a real art museum.

Art Museum Scavenger Hunt List*

- children
- a dog
- fruit
- people eating
- a celebration
- art created by a woman
- art showing an historical event
- a huge outdoor sculpture
- a piece of jewelry at least 50 years old

*Feel free to add your own ideas!

Real-Life Treasures

Otzi, Stone-Age Man

Imagine that you're hiking in the Austrian Alps with a friend. It's been a cold, tiring day, and all you can think about is getting back to your warm room and taking a hot bath. But before heading back, you see something odd. You stop. You stare . . .

In 1991, a couple hiking in the Austrian Alps stumbled on an amazing historical treasure. Ice had melted away from a glacier to uncover a man who scientists believe lived during the Stone Age. The man, named Otzi, is thought to have lived from 3350 to 3100 B.C. He was found wearing shoes made of straw and leather, clothes made of plant fiber and leather, and a cap made of brown bear fur. Scientists believe that Otzi was caught in a storm while hunting wild goats, because he was found beside a wooden backpack, a copper ax, and a leather bow with arrows. Scientists took six years to conduct more than 80 scientific studies of Otzi. Today, he is on display in an Italian museum.

Tomb of King Tutankhamen

"Boy, it's hot in here," you say to yourself. You're poking around in the ancient pyramids in Egypt. Suddenly you spot a door that's partially hidden from sight. "What could be in there?" you ask yourself . . .

During his reign of Egypt from 1333 to 1323 B.C., King Tutankhamen was an ordinary Egyptian king. However, after his death, he gave the world important information about the ways of ancient Egypt. The ancient Egyptians believed strongly in life after death, and so kings were buried with their treasures. King Tutankhamen was no different. His body was laid in three nesting coffins, the last one made of solid gold. King Tut's face was covered in a spectacular gold mask. Howard Carter discovered King Tut's tomb in 1922. Even today it is seen as one of the most important archaeological discoveries ever.

Incredible luck and hard work led to the discovery of these treasures. For more information about these and other historical treasures, search the Internet or look in an encyclopedia.

COMPREHENSION QUARTERLY

CQ

5

ISSUE D: Determining
Important Ideas and Themes

DARE to *Dream*

Dare to Dream

THINK ABOUT: Determining Important Ideas and Themes

In this issue:

DETERMINING IMPORTANT IDEAS AND THEMES

Sharing a Dream

Lan, Kabili, and Justin have always played on the vacant lots down the block. These lots are the only open land for miles, so that's where they built a fort, planted a garden, and spent their free time. Kabili and Justin were deciding what to do with their Saturday morning when Lan ran up waving the following news report:

Spotlight on Investment Corporation's Condos

Investment Corporation, a realty company and condominium developer that was founded in 1998, is headed by Grandville's own Jermaine Banks. The company has seen remarkable success in its short existence, with sales growing from just over one million dollars in its first year to more than four million this year.

"Condos are popular, and we build condominiums that have all the features buyers look for," according to Banks.

Investment Corporation's latest project, pending purchase of the property, is an eight-unit townhouse at 117 and 119 Caldwell. "We're especially excited about this development," adds Banks. "It's a great opportunity to bring much-needed housing to the area."

The kids read the article carefully to **determine the important ideas and themes** that had gotten Lan so excited. "So," Kabili said, "some developer is putting up a new condo. That's the main idea. So what?"

"Kabili, you're missing one very important detail. Look at the addresses. Those addresses are the vacant lots that we're standing on right now!" Lan replied.

The boys talked about this problem for some time. What a great dream it would be if the lots could become a small park instead of a condo development! They decided to figure out some way to convince the developer and their town council to make their dream real by building a park on the site.

Think about a time you read something that was very important to you. Your past experiences and what you already knew helped you determine the important ideas and themes in what you read.

Sarah's Secret

by Angela Shelf Medearis

My Momma and I have lived on the Butler's plantation since I was three years old. The Butlers bought us from a slave trader down in New Orleans. Momma says our people were sold into slavery in West Africa. Momma's family was separated as soon as they reached America. We've been living in Hattersville, Virginia, for the last five years.

My daddy lives on the Chancy cotton plantation about six miles away. We only get to see him on special days, like at Christmastime or during the Harvest Fest.

During the slave auction, Momma and I cried and begged Mr. Chancy to buy us, too, and not to tear our family apart. Mr. Butler heard us and tried to talk Mr. Chancy into buying us. Mr. Butler doesn't like to see slave families separated. Since Mr. Chancy didn't want me and Momma, Mr. Butler bought us. He told us that at least we wouldn't be that far away from Daddy.

What Mr. Butler doesn't seem to understand is that we don't want to be separated from Daddy—ever. We want to be free to be a family the same way he and his wife, Annie, his daughter, Lucy, and his son, Jared, are a family. Ever since the slave auction, Daddy, Mommy, and I have been thinking of ways to get our freedom. We dream about the day we can be free and be a family.

It seems like Momma sews for the Butler family from sunup to sundown every day. I help her sew on buttons and ribbons when I have time.

My main job is to serve Miss Lucy and Mr. Jared. I stay with them day and night. I even fan them while they study their lessons with their tutor, Mr. Toddman.

Miss Lucy and Mr. Jared study their lessons in the parlor. I love schooltime. Right now they're studying the geography of Virginia.

Last week, Mr. Toddman spent days teaching about the roads between Virginia and Pennsylvania.

"Why in the world do you keep going on and on about Pennsylvania?" Miss Lucy demanded crossly. "Pa says we're not ever going there. That's where the Yanks have their army."

"Everyone knows we're fighting the Civil War against the North," Mr. Jared said. "Those blue-shirt Yanks don't have a chance against our Confederate army!"

"Perhaps," Mr. Toddman said, "but it's good to know about Pennsylvania because every man, woman, and child is free there, both blacks and whites."

I was so surprised that I stopped fanning. Mr. Toddman looked at me and then looked out of the window.

"If a person knew how to get to Pennsylvania, they could find freedom there," Mr. Toddman said.

"Horsefeathers!" Miss Lucy exclaimed. "I don't want to go to Pennsylvania. I like it just fine right here in Virginia."

"Very well," sighed Mr. Toddman. "Let's do something you like to do. Let's practice our writing. Then we'll read another chapter from our book under the arbor in the garden."

Miss Lucy and Mr. Jared clapped their hands. Miss Lucy loves to write. Mr. Jared likes to read. He has a wagon load of books lining one wall of his room.

Sometimes, when the family has gone off to church or to a party, I practice my handwriting in Miss Lucy's room or crawl underneath Mr. Jared's bed and read one of his books.

What is important to remember about what you've read so far? Why do you think it's important?

Yesterday, Momma caught me reading and writing. "Sarah," Momma whispered, "just what do you think you're doing? Miss Lucy and Mr. Jared are going to be mad if they catch you playing with their things!"

"Doggone it! I'm not playing, Momma," I said. "I'm practicing my handwriting."

"Sarah," Momma glared at me, "how did you learn how to read and to write?"

"I just pay attention to what Mr. Toddman teaches Miss Lucy and Mr. Jared each day."

Momma asked me if I could keep a secret. I nodded my head yes. She asked me if I could write something for her. I carefully copied down every word she said. Momma blew on the paper until the ink was dry. Then she had me read what I'd written. She carefully folded the paper and put it into the pocket of her dress.

What do you think the author wants you to know about Sarah?

"Sarah, I don't want you to read or write anything else until I tell you to," Momma said. "It's against the law for a slave to read or write in Virginia. If you're caught, everyone in this house will be in trouble."

"I won't do anything else until you say so," I promised.

The next morning, Momma woke me up before sunup. "Happy birthday, Sarah," Momma said.

Momma gave me a tiny rag doll with a face the color of smooth, black charcoal. Her hair was made of yarn and tied with a ribbon. She was wearing a beautiful, polka-dotted dress made from a scrap leftover from Mrs. Butler's new gown.

"Oh, Momma," I cried, "she's so pretty!" I hugged the doll tightly. She crackled strangely. "What did you stuff her with?" I asked. "She feels funny."

"Don't you worry about that," Momma said. "This doll is worth her weight in gold. Take good care of her and carry her everywhere you go. She should fit right in your pocket."

"I'm going to call her Star," I said. "She's as pretty as the sky at night."

"Star is a good name for that doll—after the North Star that leads to freedom. And I've got a secret to tell you," Mamma shared. "Tonight, we're going to Pennsylvania."

"What about Daddy?" I asked. "Is he coming, too?"

"Don't you worry about your daddy," Momma said.
"You just keep Star close to you. Tonight, when the Butlers
go to that party at Mr. Chancy's house, we're going with
them. We'll help Mrs. Butler and Miss Lucy get dressed. Then
we're going to run away to Pennsylvania."

That night, when the Butler family went to Mr. Chancy's
ball, Momma and I went along. Star crackled in my pocket as
I helped button up Miss Lucy's shoes.

"What's that noise?" Miss Lucy asked.

"My doll," I said. "Her name is Star." I took Star out of
my pocket and showed her to Miss Lucy.

"What a pretty doll," Mrs. Butler said.

"I'm going to keep her," Miss
Lucy declared.

What do you
think the author
wants you to
know about the
doll, Star?

Before I knew it, Miss Lucy had
grabbed Star out of my hands. We tugged
on the doll, back and forth, back and forth.
Star's leg ripped open at the seam.

"That's Sarah's birthday present, Miss Lucy," Momma
said softly. "I'll make you a pretty doll that matches your
new dress."

"That will stop this argument," Mrs. Butler said.

"Make it right away!" Miss Lucy demanded.

Miss Lucy followed her mother down the hall to the
ballroom. As soon as they were out of sight, Momma grabbed
me by the hand. We climbed through the window and ran to
the stables. Suddenly, a man appeared from the pitch-black
shadows. He grabbed me and put his hand over my mouth.
My heart was pounding. I tried to get away, but I couldn't.

"Happy birthday, Sarah," the man whispered. "Let me see
that doll of yours."

It was Daddy! I took Star out of my pocket and gave it
to him.

We followed Daddy out of the stables. Momma
and I climbed into a wagon filled with baskets
of vegetables. We covered ourselves with a
heavy quilt. Daddy quietly guided the mare
onto the main road.

Why do you think
it's important that
Momma and Sarah
cover themselves
with a quilt?

We traveled for hours without anyone
following us. Then I heard the sound of

hoofbeats. I carefully lifted the edge of the quilt. A man on horseback was waving a lantern.

"Stop where you are!" he demanded.

It was a patroller. Patrollers are hired by slave owners to make sure no one escapes. Some slaves are allowed to travel if they have a special pass from their master. I was so afraid that I started to tremble.

"I'm on my way to the farm market in Patterly, Sir," Daddy said. "I was told to get an early start."

"Do you have a pass?" the man asked.

"Yes sir, I do," Daddy answered.

Daddy gave the man a piece of cream-colored paper. It was the paper I'd written for Momma! How did Daddy get it from her?

"You can go now," the man said. "Here's your pass."

Daddy took the pass and put it into his pocket.

We rode hour after hour, hiding by day and traveling by night. One starry night, Daddy stopped the wagon.

"Look at the sky, Sarah," Daddy said. "This is the first time you've ever seen the stars as a free child."

"We're free?" I asked.

"We're in Pennsylvania now," Daddy said, "thanks to you and Star."

"What did we do?" I asked.

"Your Momma hid that freedom pass you wrote inside Star's dress," Daddy said. "We'd never have gotten this far without it. Our dream has come true."

Daddy gave Star back to me. I hugged her tightly.

"We're free, Star," I whispered to her. "Free to be a family." ●

Are there some parts of the story that are more important to the theme? Which ones? Why?

Pass to Freedom

What was the important idea that Momma told Sarah to write on the cream-colored paper? Make the pass that Daddy handed to the patroller. Be sure to include supporting details in the note that would convince the patroller to say, "You can go now."

What If?

Sarah learned to read and write, even though as a slave, she was forbidden to. Make a list of at least ten things you do every day that you wouldn't be able to do if you were not able to read or write.

Free at Last!

Freedom was such an important dream to Sarah and her parents that they risked their lives to escape slavery. How did they feel when they looked at the stars twinkling in the night sky in Pennsylvania and knew they were free? Write a cinquain poem in which you express how Sarah and her family might have felt.

Maps to Freedom

*"The **monkey wrench** turns the **wagon wheel** toward Canada on a **bear's paw** trail to the crossroads."*

This sentence may not make sense to you. But Sarah and her family may have understood its meaning. Contained within the sentence are the names of four quilt patterns.

Patterns in quilts were used by slaves to communicate secret messages about escaping to freedom on the Underground Railroad. Nonsense sentences were used to help the slaves remember the messages and to create visual maps in their minds.

When a slave saw a quilt with an individual pattern on it hung out a window or on a fence on their plantation, they knew an escape was being planned.

Look at these patterns and read what they mean. Then use graph paper and design your own quilt pattern.

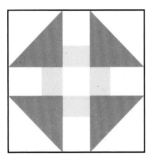

Monkey Wrench

Now is the time to gather what you need for escape. It also meant that you must be mentally prepared, too.

Wagon Wheel

It is now time to pack.

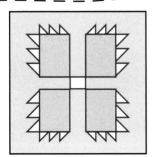

Bear's Paw

Follow the paths of bears looking for food and water through the Appalachians.

Crossroads

The destination is Cleveland, Ohio.

SEEING HANDS:
THE ART OF MICHAEL NARANJO

BY KATACHA DÍAZ

You can't miss it. A bronze sculpture of *Snake Dancer* stands gracefully on the lawn and lures you to the front entry gate of artist Michael Naranjo's studio and home on the outskirts of Santa Fe, New Mexico. The *Snake Dancer* is awesome, and it lets you know that you've arrived at a special place.

Above: Bronze of *Shar*
Right: Life-size bronze of mother bathing child

The Naranjo house is filled with an assortment of sculptures the artist has created over three decades. In the entry courtyard, a life-size sculpture of a mother and child greets visitors. Perched high up on a nearby adobe wall is a bronze sculpture of an eagle holding on tightly to a plump fish.

In the living room of the house Naranjo shares with wife, Laurie, and their two daughters, there are six original Naranjo bronze sculptures. These include *Shar,* a horse, and *Tender Moments,* a young mother with her baby strapped on her back and her *metate,* a stone grinding board, sitting close by. Outside in the back porch, another bronze eagle is suspended from a long wire and gracefully flies in the breeze.

Sculptor Michael Naranjo was born in Santa Fe, New Mexico, in 1944. He grew up in the Santa Clara Pueblo, and his family spoke Tewa, a Native American language. His father was a carpenter and his mother was a potter. "I have seven sisters and two brothers, so we had great water fights and pillow fights! There were so many of us that we had several teams competing against each other," he remembers with a mischievous smile on his face.

Naranjo explains that his deep love and respect for nature goes back to his childhood. He and his brother would frequently walk up in the mountains, enjoying the outdoors.

Naranjo is quick to point out that his artistic talent appeared during childhood when he spent time working with his hands and making things out of discarded pieces of his mother's clay. When he was nine years old, the Naranjo family moved to Taos, New Mexico, where many artists had opened galleries. "I'd walk by the galleries and see all kinds of art," Naranjo says. "I thought, someday I, too, will be an artist. I knew from an early age what I wanted to be."

> What is your purpose in reading about Michael Naranjo? How will this help you decide what's important?

When he was seventeen, Naranjo crafted a traditional Santa Clara bear out of light clay. However, for his second piece, a horse, he decided to experiment and use *micaceous* clay. "This type of clay," the artist explains, "is coarse and difficult to work with, but I saw it as a challenge. Both of these pieces reaffirmed my desire and commitment to become a sculptor." The clay horse is one of his favorite pieces, and it's prominently displayed in the entry hallway of Naranjo's home.

After high school graduation, Naranjo attended college, where he studied art and also took anatomy classes. He left college after two years and a short time later was drafted into the U.S. Army. The twenty-three-year-old Native American was sent thousands of miles away from his home in New Mexico to Vietnam.

January 8, 1968, is a date Naranjo will never forget. He was crawling like a snake across a rice paddy with his infantry platoon when Vietcong soldiers ambushed them.

"I turned around to look and remember locking eyes with the Vietcong soldier who threw the grenade into my hand. It was the last thing I saw," he says.

The grenade exploded beside Naranjo, blinding him forever. It also left him with a badly damaged right hand. Naranjo was taken to a military hospital in Japan for medical care and surgery. "My pinkie was amputated. The ring finger was dead on one side, so I have no feeling. If I cut it, I can't feel it. There I was, lying in the hospital bed, and I thought about my childhood dream to become a sculptor. I thought to myself, kiss that one goodbye."

One day a volunteer stopped by to talk with Naranjo, and he asked her to bring him some clay. "My right arm was tied down," he remembers. "I only had my left hand free and I couldn't see anymore. I took a little piece of clay,

> What do you think the author wants you to know about Michael's injuries?

Above: Michael and Laurie Naranjo
Right: Naranjo carries *Ram Dancer* back to his studio

rolled it up, and I made an inchworm. Then I made a goldfish. I knew they looked OK because people could tell what they were. The minute I made that inchworm, I knew I could do it, and all it would take is time."

Sitting in his Santa Fe studio, Naranjo leans over a small block of brown wax. He uses a small hairdryer to soften the wax to make it easier to handle. Naranjo doesn't use any tools to sculpt his pieces. Instead, his long, sensitive fingers explore the wax while he depends on his hands to do the seeing. "I use my right hand to hold the piece of wax in place. My fingers and fingernails are my sculpting tools, and my hands touch and do the seeing."

The wax sculpture he will make today, Naranjo says, was inspired a few days ago while he and Laurie were driving back home from the grocery store in Santa Fe. His fingers begin to explore the shapeless piece of wax. He begins the process of creating the small figure of a Native American man— his body, the head, his arms, and legs. Eventually when the artist finishes this piece, it will be enlarged and cast into bronze.

Naranjo sculpts in total darkness, but it's what his heart feels and sees that he shapes with his hand. The artist truly has a remarkable inner vision—a sixth sense. This allows him to see pictures in his mind of things he had once seen and experienced when he wasn't blind.

Ninety-eight percent of the time, Naranjo uses wax for his pieces. His style is simple and straightforward. His sculptures are graceful, powerful, and unique, and they tell a story. The pieces range in size from 3 inches to 9 feet tall. Some are specially-commissioned, one-of-a-kind sculptures, and others are made in limited amounts. The sculptures range in price from $400 to $67,000.

What do you think are the most important things to know about how Naranjo sculpts?

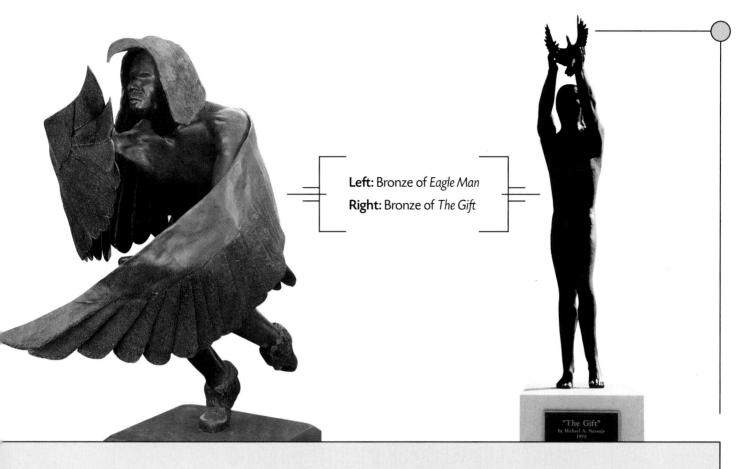

Left: Bronze of *Eagle Man*
Right: Bronze of *The Gift*

Naranjo's sculptures show a variety of subjects, including animals, Native American figures, Santa Clara Pueblo dancers, children, and religious figures. Naranjo's favorite piece, he says, is always the one he's creating and working on at that time. "A piece can take me hours, days, weeks, or months to complete. It all depends on how inspired I am and how much time I put into it. I have no set schedule," he explains.

Over the years, Naranjo's sculptures have won numerous awards and honors. In 1999, he was the recipient of the LIFE Foundation's Presidential Unsung Hero Award in Washington, DC. That year Michael was also the recipient of the National Commander's Award and named Outstanding Disabled Veteran of the Year by the Disabled American Veterans.

Naranjo's sculptures can be seen in public places. Some are at the White House, in the Vatican, at the New Mexico State Library,

and at the state capital building in Santa Fe. His work is shown at galleries and museums around the world. In fact, many of his sculptures are sent on special "touch tours," where both visually impaired and sighted people are invited to touch his beautiful works of art. "I want everyone to run their hands over my pieces," Naranjo says. "This really means so much to them, and I'm speaking from personal experience because I feel the same way."

Michael Naranjo's inner strength and self-determination helped him to follow his dream to become a sculptor who sees with his hands. "Yesterday helped me get to today," he says. "Tomorrow I don't want to know about. I learned first how to be a sculptor. I just happen to be Native American. Then I just happen to be a blind man." ●

If you remember two important ideas about Michael Naranjo, what would they be?

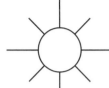

Stop and Respond

IN THE NEWS

Make a list of five headlines that might have appeared in newspapers through the years about Michael Naranjo. Then pick one of the headlines and write the news story to go with it.

PUTTING YOUR STAMP ON MICHAEL NARANJO

Design a stamp to honor the life of Michael Naranjo. Create a stamp that expresses your point of view as to what is most important about his life.

CAUGHT IN THE WEB OF COURAGE

Would you describe Michael Naranjo as courageous? Why or why not? Use a web to show the details in the article that support your opinion. When you're through, compare your web to a classmate's.

THANKS, MICHAEL!

Write a letter to Michael Naranjo. Tell him what you learned from reading the article about overcoming obstacles in life.

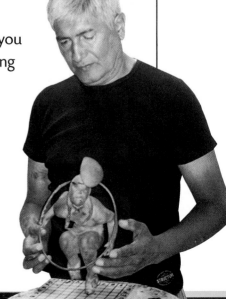

Renaissance *Dreamer*

Leonardo da Vinci 1452–1519

Leonardo da Vinci was a man of many talents. He was a painter, inventor, researcher, scientist, architect, and engineer. He was very smart and closely observed the world around him.

Leonardo dreamed of flying and of machines made for transportation. Designs for inventions were found in his notebooks. They included a helicopter, diving suit, bicycle, submarine, hang glider, spring-driven automobile, and parachute. He envisioned many other inventions, too.

Leonardo made all of his notes in mirror writing. No one knows exactly why he did this. However, it is known that Leonardo was left-handed. By writing backward, his hand did not smudge the wet ink. Mirror writing also lent secrecy to his writings. Many of Leonardo's ideas were about things that were forbidden or not accepted at the time.

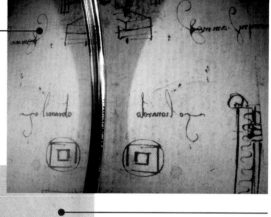

Adrian Nicholas made a canvas parachute using Leonardo's fifteenth century design and made a successful jump over South Africa in June 2000.

DETERMINING IMPORTANT IDEAS AND THEMES

Keeping the Dream Alive

At the start of every workday, Jermaine Banks reads the important mail his secretary has set aside for him. This morning, a letter from a group of kids caught his eye. He read the letter carefully to **determine the important ideas and themes** and what special meaning they may have for him.

Dear Mr. Banks:

We know you remember what it is like to be a kid without many places to play because we found out that you used to live in our neighborhood when you were young. We bet you remember how much fun it was to play in the vacant lots at 117 and 119 Caldwell because it is the only empty land around. We've got a great fort on the land, and we even planted a garden this year. Want some tomatoes? Just stop by, and we'll be glad to share some with you.

We are writing to you about an article we saw in the paper the other day. It said that you were thinking of building condos on the property. We want to ask you not to do this. Where will we play? We don't have any parks or open land. Our neighborhood doesn't need condos. It needs parks! Can't you donate the land to the city to build a playground? Please consider our request.

Respectfully,
Kabili, Lan, and Justin

Jermaine Banks had received other letters about this same theme, but he'd never gotten one from a group of kids. Because of his background, he knew that the kids were right—there was no park in their neighborhood. The vacant lots were the only empty land for miles. He thought for a while. Then he reached for the phone.

When you read the next story, your prior knowledge and past experiences will help you better understand what is happening.

Drawn into the future

by Elaine Kule

Leon sat up in bed, needing a moment to decide if he had been dreaming. Of course he had been. He put his head back on his pillow, trying to remember it all. He had visited a strange, new world. It was a world of the future. It was a world controlled by robots.

What an incredible place! There were moving sidewalks and cars that flew. Buses and trucks ran along tri-level roads. Telephone booths with video screens let callers see who they were talking to. Computer stations were on every corner.

Because robots have no emotions, anger and jealousy were outlawed. Hatred and fighting were banned. There wasn't any theft because everyone lived in the same kind of housing and owned the same amount of property. Even clothing was identical for robots and humans. Everyone wore gray uniforms and silver boots.

Leon stretched and slipped out of bed. His parents were still sleeping, so he quietly washed, put on jeans and a T-shirt, and helped himself to breakfast. Then he sat at his desk and took out a sheet of paper and a sharpened pencil. He began to sketch what he dreamed so he wouldn't forget it.

Leon loved drawing. With quick, flowing strokes, he drew the place he had visited. Leon wondered if this could be the world of the future. He grabbed some felt-tip pens and brought his picture to life using bold, bright colors. He even gave two robots red, orange, and yellow clothing.

What do you think the author wants you to know about Leon?

Suddenly, a narrow column of brilliant light arose from the paper. Leon was so shocked that he dropped the pen he was holding. For some reason, he looked at the clock on his nightstand. It was six-thirty. A loud "whoosh" sound got his attention. Instantly, Leon was pulled into the beam of light. He slid down a tunnel so fast that when he landed on his feet, he was nearly breathless.

"Where am I?" he wondered, looking all around. Then he recognized his surroundings. It was the picture he had drawn! He had somehow, magically, fallen into it. He even saw people wearing the outfits he'd given them.

"How did this happen?" Leon asked aloud. He knew that he must look silly, talking to himself, but he didn't care. "Am I dreaming again?"

"No, you're not dreaming," one of the robots said. "You've entered a very real world, the world of the future. Welcome."

Two guards appeared out of nowhere. "Hello," one of them said, "my name is Sigmund and this is Henrietta. We hope you had a pleasant journey."

"Will you come with us, please?" Henrietta invited. "Our leader wants to meet you."

"Fine with me," Leon said. He didn't want to show fear. If I can draw myself into this place, I can somehow draw myself out, he thought. Besides, he was curious. How many people had the chance to see the future?

Leon was led over a white line, which he quickly realized was the edge of his paper. He was instantly brought into a bigger world, one beyond his imagination. He saw huge buildings, gigantic stores, and robots of every shape and size. Yet, although everyone seemed polite, there wasn't a smile, laugh, or frown to be seen or heard.

While following his escorts, Leon passed a human family. He immediately thought of his parents, who would be getting up any minute. They would be upset and worried to find him missing. He looked around for a telephone booth. Then he remembered that he was in the

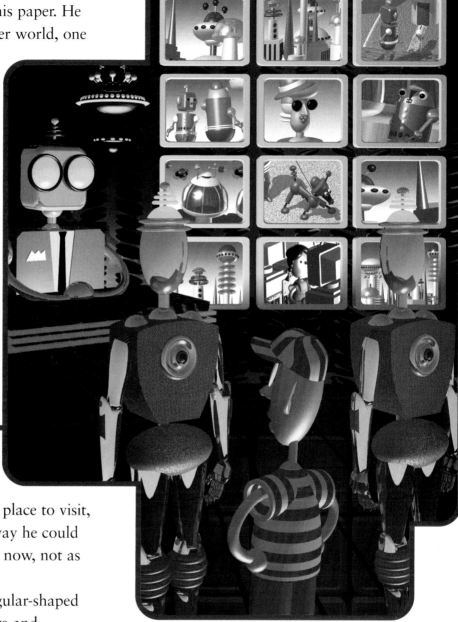

future. He could hardly call people who were living in the past. This might be an interesting place to visit, Leon realized, but there was no way he could spend any time here. At least, not now, not as a ten-year-old.

The guards led him to a triangular-shaped building that had triangular doors and windows. They walked to a rocket-shaped elevator and stepped inside. After reaching the top floor in about two seconds, the group entered a gigantic room. Its walls had screens and video monitors that showed every part of the world. At the front of the room was a large desk. Behind it was a short robot with a loud, mechanical-sounding voice. "Hello, Leon. It's nice to meet such a talented, young artist."

"Thank you," Leon said. "What's your name? And how did you know mine?"

"My name is Igor. I'm the leader of this world, and it's my job to know everything that goes on in it. For example, when some of our citizens suddenly wear colorful clothes, well, that's something I was told about right away. In fact, that's why you're here. We can't have that, Leon. You'll have to change everything back to the way it was."

What does the author want you to know about Leon's trip to the future?

"But why?" Leon asked. "Color is good. And not everyone should wear the same clothing. People need choices."

"I disagree," Igor replied. "In your day, people had too much to choose from. They wasted time and money deciding what to wear. Some people had more clothing than others. This caused bad feelings. We have a safe, orderly world here. You mustn't change it."

"I'll do as you ask, " Leon said. "I just need to get home. My parents will worry about me."

"Time has stood still in your world," Igor said. "Look at the screen behind you."

Leon turned and saw a view of his room. The clock on his night table still read six-thirty.

"Our scientists have found a way to control time," Igor said. "But unfortunately, the next transport to your world doesn't leave for another hour. Why don't you see one of our schools and visit a nearby family? You may find it interesting."

"Thanks, I will," Leon said. He, Henrietta, and Sigmund rode in the rocket-like elevator down to the first floor and stepped onto the moving sidewalk. Within moments, they were in front of a glass building.

"Here we are," Henrietta said as the electric-eye door flew open. "This school is first-rate. I think you'll like it."

Leon entered the brand-new building. He saw robots in the doorways of each classroom. Children were quietly working at the computers on their desks. What he didn't see were teachers. He looked at the guards.

"We have teachers observing the children through video cameras," Sigmund explained, as if reading his mind. "The students' work is checked and corrected by computer."

Leon searched the children's faces. Each one was staring at a computer screen or tapping at a keyboard in the silent room. They all looked busy, but not very happy.

"Well, we'd better leave if you're to meet a family and make your transport in time," Henrietta said. They left the school, crossed the

What experiences have you had that help you understand what you're reading?

street, and hopped onto the electronic steps of a gray house. A door opened instantly. On the other side was a robot.

"Hello. My name is George. Enter." As they stepped inside, Leon noticed a video screen of two sleeping babies.

"Are their parents at home?" Leon asked the guards in a whisper.

"No, babies are cared for by robots during most of the day," Sigmund said. "Parents and other humans are too busy to look after children."

"Wow," Leon said. This life in the future may be exciting in some ways. But there was a lot that didn't seem right to him. People were cut off from their feelings and from one another. If this was the best way to

improve human behavior, it struck Leon as sad.

Someone had to warn people of what could happen if they didn't treat each other better, Leon thought. Someone had to remind people to choose their leaders carefully, or others may one day believe that robots will do a better job. Someone had to do all of these things to keep the wonderful advances of the future and save what was good in the present. Maybe that someone was him.

"I think I've seen enough," Leon said to the guards.

"Very well," Henrietta replied. "Your transport should be here anyway."

They brought him back to his picture where a column of bright light awaited him. "Good-bye, Sigmund and Henrietta," Leon said.

"Have a safe trip home," they said in return.

Leon entered the band of light. In seconds, he heard a "whoosh" sound. He was back in his room just as the clock struck 6:31.

"Are you up, Leon?" he heard his mother call out.

"Yes, Mom," he answered. He ran to the hallway and gave her a big hug. ●

Are there some parts of the story more important to the theme? Which ones? Why?

Stop and Respond

Dash into 2100

On your mark! Get set! Use your imagination and dash into the year 2100! What do you see? What do you hear? Draw a picture showing a scene from life in 2100. Then write a caption for your picture describing your futuristic scene.

Drawn into Poetry

A triplet is a three-line poem in which all the lines rhyme. Write a triplet poem about Leon's dream. Share your poem with classmates.

You and Leon

You've read about Leon in the science fiction story, "Drawn into the Future." Think about how Leon's life relates to your own life. What similarities do you recognize between your life and Leon's life? How is his life different from yours? Make a list of five ways that Leon's life is similar to your own and five ways that it is different.

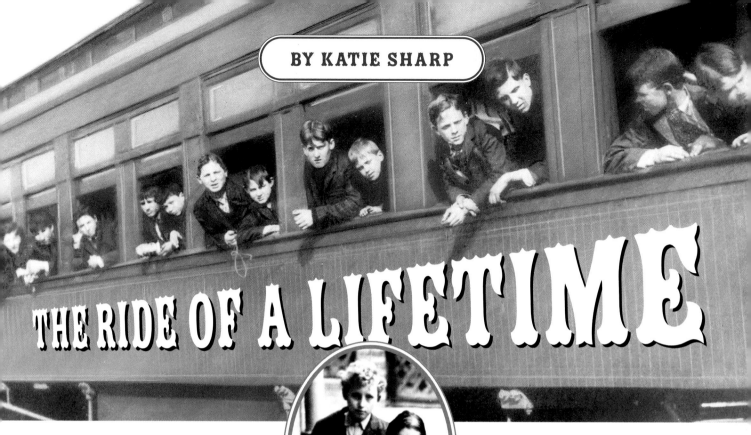

BY KATIE SHARP

THE RIDE OF A LIFETIME

THE ORPHAN TRAINS

In September 1854, a train chugged into a small town in southwest Michigan. It was a train like no other the town had ever seen. Its passengers were wide-eyed youngsters who had been rescued from the streets of New York City and brought to America's West in search of living their dreams of a better life. Over the next 75 years, many similar trains would follow. They would come to be known as Orphan Trains.

WHY THERE WERE ORPHANS

The United States was growing quickly in the 1850s. Posters and flyers spread across Europe and other countries promoting the promise of America. Soon, thousands of immigrants flooded New York City and other port cities in America in search of a new life. Much to their surprise, however, there weren't a lot of jobs. When work was available, it paid very little. In time, many immigrant and American families found themselves with little or no money. They were forced to live in overcrowded buildings.

Times were hard. Many young families fell apart. One or both parents often became sick and died from the unhealthy living conditions. Others died in

What is your purpose for reading about the Orphan Trains? How will this help you decide what is important?

accidents on their jobs. Mothers and fathers were left alone to care for their young children. Many simply couldn't do it. They had no other choice but to find other places for their children to live.

Orphanages were built to care for as many children as possible. Often, however, they had to close their doors to more children because they had no more room. A number of children found themselves living on the streets of New York. They were dirty, poor, and hungry. They were forced to be self-sufficient. They begged for food and money. Some worked jobs selling matches or newspapers. Some danced and sang on street corners for money. But they made very little money. At night, they slept huddled together with other homeless children wherever they could find shelter.

> What ideas and experiences help you understand what you're reading?

MR. BRACE MAKES A DIFFERENCE

In 1853, Charles Loring Brace, a young minister from a well-to-do Connecticut family, arrived in New York City to work with the poor. He was horrified by the number of homeless children prowling the streets. He talked with them face-to-face. He decided he had to do something to help them.

At that time, America was quickly expanding west. In fact, four railroads had been planned to carry people and goods to America's heartland. Mr. Brace knew that the farmers settling in the west needed workers to help them build their farms. He believed that they would welcome New York's homeless children. He thought the farmers could give the children not only work, but that they would treat them as new sons and daughters. With plenty of food, a family, and clean air to breathe, Mr. Brace thought these children could become self-reliant grown-ups. His dream was to send thousands of New York's children to America's farmlands.

Soon, Mr. Brace and a group of his well-to-do friends began a new organization. They called it the Children's Aid Society. The Society was set up to raise money, arrange trips, and obtain the permission needed to move the children to new homes. Thousands of children came or were brought to the Children's Aid Society. There were cheerful boys wanting to go West to the land of the cowboys; there were girls—ragged and barefoot. And there were children brought in by down-on-their-luck fathers and mothers who could no longer care for them.

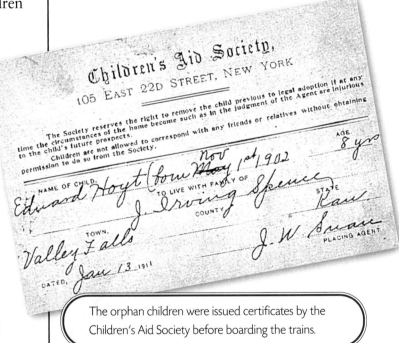

The orphan children were issued certificates by the Children's Aid Society before boarding the trains.

ALL ABOARD THE ORPHAN TRAINS

About three times a month, Mr. Brace's children traveled by train in groups of 30 or 40 and sometimes many more. Railroads were the most inexpensive way to move the children westward. They were accompanied by agents of the Children's Aid Society— men and women who worked with Mr. Brace. And while many of the children didn't know it, they were beginning an unforgettable journey to a new life far away from the filth and hunger of New York City's streets. Many of them were excited and anxious to meet their new families. Others were fearful and upset. They had no idea where they were going or what to expect. The agents tried to comfort the children by speaking of the good homes that awaited them.

The train trip usually lasted from three or four days to a full week. There were a number of stops along the way. And each town knew the Orphan Train was coming because flyers and ads had been posted to announce its arrival.

As a stop came near, the children changed their clothes and washed their faces. They had to look their best if they wanted to be chosen. The children would leave the train and appear

WANTED!
HOMES FOR CHILDREN

A company of homeless children from the East will arrive at LEBA-NON, MISSOURI, on

Thursday, December 30, '09

These children are of various ages and of both sexes, having been thrown friendless upon the world. They come under the auspices of the Children's Aid Society, of New York. These children are well disciplined, having come from the various orphanages. The citizens of this community are asked to assist the agent in finding good homes for them. Persons taking these children must be recommended by the local committee. They must treat the children in every way as members of the family, sending them to school, church, Sabbath school and properly clothe them until they are 18 years old. The following well known citizens have agreed to act as a local committee to aid agents in securing homes:

| W. I. Wallace | J. W. Farris | J. G. Lingsweiler |
| E. B. Kellerman | Sam Farrar | Dr. J. M. Billings |

Applications must be made to, and indorsed by, the local committee. An address will be given by the agent. Come and see the children and hear the address. Distribution will take place at the OPERA HOUSE, Thursday, December 30, at 10 a. m. and 2 p. m.

B. W. TICE, MISS A. L. HILL, Agents, 105 E. 22nd St., New York City
J. W. SWAN, University Place, Neb., Western Agent.

Above: Advertisements like this were posted throughout the Midwest.

Below: This group of orphan girls were given dolls for the train ride.

on a stage, which was often set up in front of the town's meeting hall or a church. The agent told the audience a little bit about each child— the child's age, background, and special skills. If a family wanted a certain child, the child had the right to refuse to go. But if the child agreed, the new parents signed some papers and took their new child home. If later on, the child was not happy in the new home, he or she could leave. In their new homes, children were expected to work as members of the household. In return, the new parents were asked to provide a home, food, and an education, just as they would for their own children.

What do you think the author wants you to know about the Orphan Train?

Children whom no one picked got back on the train and traveled to the next stop. While most children were happy to be chosen, they were also scared and confused. Frequently, brothers and sisters were separated. A sister might be picked on one stop, leaving her brother to board the train without her.

Some of the orphan children were adopted to help on family farms.

Not just any family was allowed to take a child from an Orphan Train. The Children's Aid Society asked each town along the train route to choose a group of citizens who could approve families before the train arrived. The group usually included a minister, banker, doctor, teacher, store owner, and others. The group met one-on-one with interested families. The Children's Aid Society allowed only those families who had been approved by the group to take children from the train.

In the years to come, the Children's Aid Society found homes for some 100,000 youngsters. Other child-saving organizations, such as the New York Foundling Hospital, followed with their own Orphan Trains. Between 1854 and 1900, nearly 200,000 children rode the Orphan Trains. Children found homes in states from Michigan to Texas to Kansas and Minnesota. What began as one man's dream for thousands of homeless children became a great success. Many of the orphans grew up to find good jobs and to start families of their own. Of course, there were some orphans who never felt at home with their new families. Some of them ran away. And some children were not treated well by their new families. But compared to the numbers of children who were placed, there were few failures. Most Orphan Train riders became honest, hard-working citizens, just as Mr. Brace had predicted.

The Orphan Trains stopped running in the early 1900s for many reasons. A big reason was that America's view of childhood was changing. People were beginning to see that children needed time to play. Using children as workers was becoming a thing of the past. People also were starting to feel that needy families should be kept together. Laws were passed to help mothers and children make it on their own.

After reading the article, what are two important ideas to remember? Why do you think that?

On May 31, 1929, the Children's Aid Society sent three boys to a small town in Texas. It was the last of the Orphan Trains. ●

PORTRAIT OF AN ORPHAN TRAIN TRAVELER

Imagine a child who traveled on the September 1854, Orphan Train. Draw a portrait of the boy or girl and write his or her name at the top of the portrait. Then write a paragraph telling about the Orphan Train traveler's age, background, and special skills.

ORPHAN TRAIN JOURNAL

You are a newspaper reporter from New York in 1855. Your assignment is to travel on an Orphan Train and keep a journal to share with the people back home. Write a journal entry from one of the days of your trip. Share what you write with your classmates

HELP THE CHILDREN

Role-play a social worker from the Children's Aid Society. Give a fund-raising speech to persuade people to donate money to organize an Orphan Train. Present as many persuasive arguments as you can to convince people to give to this worthy cause.

List Top Ten Dream Jobs

Would your dream job be playing for a professional sports team, singing to a large crowd at an outdoor concert, photographing underwater life, or something else? Make a list of what you consider to be the top ten dream jobs and your reasons for selecting these jobs.

Helping Others

Mr. Brace decided to make a difference in the lives of homeless children by helping them find homes, and he persuaded others to help, too. Think about a relevant problem in your community and how people can help. Then design a poster in which you persuade others to help out.

Make a Sandwich Poem

Tell what you learned about someone or something from your reading by adding the missing "ingredients" to the sandwich writing pattern below—the first and last lines are the same, with the middle lines adding details.

The important thing about _____ is _____.

He/She/It is _____

And _____

And _____

And _____

But the important thing about _____ is _____.

More Books

Hesse, Karen. *Letters from Rifka*. Puffin, 1993.

MacDonald, Fiona. *The World in the Time of Leonardo da Vinci*. Chelsea House, 2000.

McMullan, Kate H. *The Story of Harriet Tubman, Conductor of the Underground Railroad*. Yearling Books, 1991.

Mochizuki, Ken. *Passage to Freedom: The Sugihara Story*. Lee & Low Books, 1997.

Nixon, Joan Lowery. *A Family Apart*. Laureleaf, 1996.

Warren, Andrea. *Orphan Train Rider: One Boy's True Story*. Houghton, 1996.

Winter, Jeanette. *Diego*. Knopf, 1994.

On the Web

Dare to Dream
http://www.myhero.com

Orphan Trains
http://www.tbox.com/isgs/projects/
    orphan-train.html
http://www.pbs.org/wgbh/amex/orphan

Underground Railroad
http://www.nationalgeographic.com/
    features/99/railroad

Exploring Leonardo
http://www.mos.org/sln/Leonardo/
    LeoHomePage.html

Across the Curriculum

Science/Technology

Could a robot pet be the most popular pet of the future? How would you feel about having a robot pet? Make a list of the pros and cons of having a live pet and a metal robot pet.

Art

What does freedom mean to you? Look through some old magazines and cut out pictures, words, or phrases that you feel capture the spirit of freedom. Use what you cut out to make a freedom collage.

Dreams are the Stories

Edison dreamed of electrifying moments.
Jules Verne dreamed of traveling to the future.
Shakespeare dreamed of speaking with many voices.
Martin Luther King dreamed of being free at last.

Dreams are the stories
We tell ourselves.

They are the flights
Of the highest soaring bird,
The songs of
Spring-fed rivers.

They are the rumble
Of the darkest tornado,
Each is a hidden door.

And behind each door
Is the beauty of imagination
Waiting . . .

When a dream comes to visit, make it comfortable;
Treat it with kindness, like a good friend,
And it will take you on adventures
Lasting a lifetime.